CHINA'S ETHNIC GROUPS AND RELIGIONS

ZHENG QIAN

Translated by Hou Xiaocui, Rong Xueqin & Huang Ying

CHINA INTERCONTINENTAL PRESS

图书在版编目（CIP）数据

中国民族与宗教：英文 / 郑茜著；侯晓萃，戎雪勤，黄颖译 . —北京：五洲传播出版社，2010.1

ISBN 978-7-5085-1685-1

I. ① 中 ... II. ① 郑… ② 侯… ③ 戎… ④ 黄… III. ① 民族政策－中国－英文 ② 宗教政策－中国－英文 IV. ① D63

中国版本图书馆 CIP 数据核字 (2009) 第 191072 号

总 顾 问／王　晨
总 策 划／王仲伟
总 监 制／郭长建
出 版 人／李向平
主　　编／吴　伟

中国民族与宗教

著　　者／郑　茜
翻　　译／侯晓萃　戎雪勤　黄　颖
责任编辑／苏　谦
装帧设计／田　林　傅晓斌
制　　作／北京原色印象文化艺术中心
图片提供／中国新闻图片网　中国日报新闻图片网　视觉中国　东方 IC
出版发行／五洲传播出版社（北京市海淀区北小马厂 6 号　邮编：100038）
电　　话／8610 － 58891281（发行部）
网　　址／www.cicc.org.cn
承 印 者／北京博海升彩色印刷有限公司
版　　次／2010 年 1 月第 1 版第 1 次印刷
开　　本／787×1092 毫米　1/16
定　　价／96.00 元

Foreword

Through its reform and opening to the outside world, China has worked an economic miracle and boosted its comprehensive strength, enhancing its standing in the international community. As more and more people around the world are eager to know and understand China, we have compiled the China Series, aiming to provide a shortcut for readers to get the basic facts about this country.

The 12 titles in this series cover China's geography, history, politics, economy, culture, law, diplomacy, national defense, and society, as well as its science, technology and education; its environment; and its ethnic groups and religions. These writings will help readers acquire a basic knowledge of China.

It is our hope that this series will enable readers to get a general idea about China:

Chinese history, culture and civilization, which is the oldest continuous major civilization in the world;

China's basic conditions—the world's largest developing country with a huge population, a country that is developing unevenly on a poor economic base; in light of these conditions, China is following its own path to sustainable development while learning from other civilizations; and

China's future—led by the Chinese Communist Party, the Chinese people are focusing their efforts on economic development and carrying on reform and opening-up; they are building a harmonious society in their own country and working for a harmonious world with lasting peace and common prosperity.

We expect that through these books our readers will begin a new journey of discovery—understanding China.

January 2010

Contents

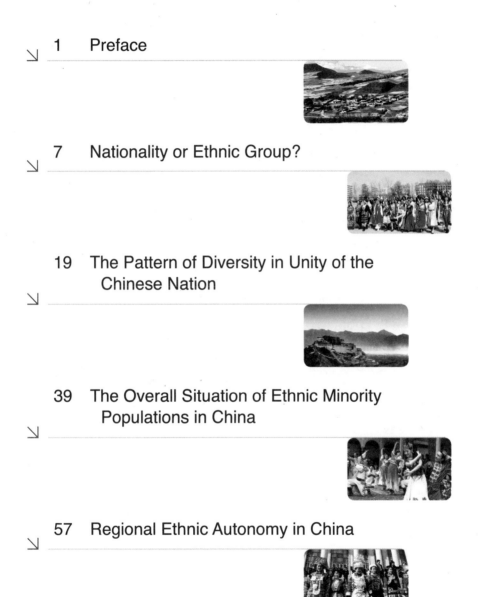

Preface

As a brief introduction to the ethnic groups and religions in China, this book has to leave out many events and people. Instead, it gives a concise elaboration and some relevant numbers.

I am deeply grateful that as a journalist that has worked on minority news reports for over 20 years, I have had opportunities to know the events that show a sense of history and to be in contact with people who promote progress. In this process, I realize, perhaps more deeply than others, that those who really speak about history are the ones that are likely to be submerged by it.

Therefore, along with the faithful and concise elaboration in the main body of this book, I think telling a story here may be a helpful addition.

In 1950, the invincible and victorious troops of the Chinese People's Liberation Army came to a stop at the foot of the A-Wa Mountain in Yunnan Province.

The troops had received an order from the Southwestern Bureau of the Central Committee of the Chinese Communist Party to suspend the march until they determined the situation in the ethnic region and won the support of ethnic minority peoples there.

A-Wa Mountain held a compact of communities of the Va minority. La Meng was a remarkably respected headman who had led his people against both British troops and later the Japanese invasion. He was a man with a lot of self esteem.

La Meng observed the Chinese People's Liberation Army camped outside A-Wa Mountain closely. He expected gunshots, but instead an ethnic work group came and invited him to participate in a delegation to watch the National Day Parade in Beijing.

This proud headman told his guests frankly: "We fought Britons when they invaded. We fought Japanese when they invaded. We also fought Kuomintang. Now comes the Liberation Army and I haven't discerned yet."

He was not lying. Over the last 100 years, wars on A-Wa Mountain had always been caused by outsiders, including British, Japanese and Kuomintang troops that looted mineral resources and occupied the land.

In order to celebrate the first anniversary of the founding of the PRC, the central government decided to invite ethnic representatives to watch the parade in Beijing. At that time, it was not clear yet how many ethnic groups there were in China, but the central government demanded that "not a single ethnic group or a representative figure should be left out."

In other places, it was a great honor for many people to visit Beijing. On the A-Wa Mountain, however, none of the 18 headmen wanted or agreed to go to Beijing.

After patient and repeated efforts by the ethnic work group, La Meng changed his attitude. He decided to use *Da Jigua* to tell the fortune in accordance with the traditional religion of the Va minority. *Da Jigua* is a practice in which many small bamboo sticks are placed in a tiny hole in a piece of chicken bone and the different patterns woven by these sticks convey different messages.

He got a string of bad omens until one day he got a lucky one, so he made up his mind to go. But the moment he stepped out of door, he saw a bird overhead flying in the opposite direction. He stopped immediately: "The bird has conveyed the god's message to us that this journey is extremely ominous and I should not go!"

La Meng closed his door again. However, the work group waited for him patiently. Where there is a will, there is a way. At last, La Meng agreed to go.

The sacred wooden drums of the Va minority were played for La Meng. But this time, what kind of rhyme should these drums play—for campaigns, for alarms, or for festivals? The rhyme played for La Meng was ambiguous and unclear. This had never happened before. Who could tell whether La Meng should leave or not?

La Meng first walked on foot, then rode horses, then took trucks and finally planes. On the plane he was dizzy and sick. When he arrived in Beijing at last he thought he was ill. Then the notice came that Premier Zhou Enlai was to invite them to dinner!

As if a stream of lifeblood was injected into his body, his illness seemed not that terrible any more. "I will go, I will go!" That night, he saw Premier Zhou. What an affable and kind person! Premier Zhou paid great respect to every ethnic representative present. La Meng had never seen a "high-level" official who was so affable.

The National Day Parade started on time on October 1st. In the ethnic delegation to watch the parade, 34 were ethnic headmen of various ethnic groups in Yunnan Province. What a splendid and exciting scene! The army passed by; the navy passed by; when an enormous sound came from the sky, La Meng looked up and saw the fighters of the Chinese People's Liberation Army.

He was shocked. This once poor and disunited country was already completely different. He burst into tears.

On the platform, La Meng suddenly felt that he was also the master of this country.

Soon the day came when they were to meet Chairman Mao. After paying their tribute, every ethnic representative went onto the platform and shook hands with Chairman

Mao.

Chairman Mao's palm was so wide and soft! It left a deep impression engraved in the mind of La Meng, headman of the Va minority.

After saying farewell to Beijing, La Meng visited Shanghai, Wuhan and Chongqing along with other members of the ethnic minority delegation, and then came back to Yunnan.

Instead of going straight back home, La Meng went to attend a delegation conference of ethnic solidarity held in Pu'er. At the conference, he and another headman Li Bao made a joint proposal: in order to achieve the everlasting solidarity of all ethnic groups, we should always follow the lead of the Communist Party of China! According to old Va minority customs, we should take an oath!

Oath-taking is a folk tradition with a long history. As a credit guarantee of personal relations, oath-taking sets up a self-disciplined system in a worship culture. When facing important events or serious disputes, people tend to build a solid relation of mutual-trust by taking oaths before the gods.

All the delegates from southern Yunnan Province received this proposal warmly and immediately decided that an oath ceremony be held in Pu'er city.

The oath ceremony of the Va minority in which an ox was slaughtered and sacrificed was very grand, solemn and mysterious. La Meng was unanimously elected as the ox slaughterer by all the delegates.

The oath ceremony was held on December 26th 1950. All the delegates from 26 ethnic communities—including subgroups—from 15 counties of Pu'er gathered in Hong Chang.

According to old Va tradition, if the ox falls over to the south after being killed, it is auspicious; if it topples over to the north, it is an omen of failure for the oath. In that case, the ceremony should not proceed and all agreements should be canceled.

To the accompaniment of wooden drums, La Meng, although in his 60s, displayed consummate skills. He stabbed the ox right in the vital point in his first try.

All the people watched the ox stumbling around, eager to know the outcome. Finally, the ox fell to the south as it was hoped and the crowd burst into thunderous acclaim.

Afterwards, La Meng and other delegates agreed to write down the "oath of solidarity" on a piece of red paper with every person's signature. Then a monument was set up.

That is the "Monument of Ethnic Solidarity." The inscription is still very clear after more than half a century. It says that:

On behalf of all ethnic minorities in Pu'er, we, delegates from 26 ethnic groups, hereby have taken an oath by stabbing the ox and drinking the sacred water, to unite together under the leadership of the Communist Party of China and devote ourselves to building a great nation of equality, freedom and happiness.

Back at home, La Meng told his fellow villagers: Ximeng is merely a tiny place compared with the vast land of the whole country. Only by following the government and the Communist Party of China can we have a bright future.

We are able to truly understand the logic of history thanks to its richness and vividness. The above story gives us a glimpse of how the new government won the trust of ethnic minorities with its sincerity, respect and equal treatment 60 years ago, and inspired their hope for a brand new future after almost a century of colonial invasions, wars, social chaos and impoverished lives since the Opium War.

In history, Chinese ethnic groups have always taken national unity as the highest political ideal and value pursuit. The People's Republic of China has resumed this historical value and won itself a brand new future.

The story may serve as the starting line to understand contemporary Chinese ethnic groups and religions. From here, you can begin your exploration into the general historical elaboration in this book.

Nationality or Ethnic Group?

A Historical Deviation

For China, a five-thousand-year-old civilization, the Opium War in 1848 can be described as a gigantic axe that brutally split Chinese history and culture. As Western modernity flooded in all at once from then on, China also entered its own modern history. Everything in the country began to change at the dawning of this period of time.

A major part of modern Chinese history has seen the absorption of Western culture, either consciously or unconsciously. In the late 19th century, Chinese people hastily accepted a variety of Western concepts, among which was the term "nation" or "nationality." A study of the introduction of this Western terminology enables us to learn how Chinese combine Western modernity with their own traditions amid misconception and tortuousness.

Natio is originally a Latin word meaning birthplace or biological descent. In the 18th century, when the European bourgeoisie began to rise quickly, the emerging class upgraded the ancient Latin word to nation with the meaning of "a common language, region, economic life (common tariff) and culture." It was used as a powerful weapon against the feudal system. In 1789, Augustine Barlow, a French missionary, first used the word nationalism to refer to a social force "that overthrows the feudal monarchial regime." Under the slogan of "One Nation, One State," the emerging Bourgeoisie successfully launched a series of social revolutions. When Bourgeois revolutions in Europe ended in 1871, a group of monoethnic states had been founded. In this sense, the words "nation" and "state" finally became one concept in modern European history.

When referring to the "nation-state" theory of the modern West, it should be noted that its core concept—"nation"—takes the shape of a state.

European capitalism subsequently began colonial conquests around the world and thus spread the "nation-state" theory beyond Europe. However, China had already been a unified multiethnic country for two thousand years when this notion entered. What sort of deviation would occur if the concept of nation and the "nation-state" theory, born in the modern West, was transplanted into China's historical and cultural background?

In fact, China's bourgeois revolution also tried to use Western theories and ideas of nationalism to launch a popular movement for national salvation. But the Chinese bourgeoisie encountered the problem of the *minzu* (ethnic group).

The main enemy facing the bourgeois revolution in modern

China has been a unified multi-ethnic country since ancient times, and thus far 56 ethnic groups have been identified.

China was the government under the rule of the Manchu nobility of the Qing Dynasty (1616–1911). In other words, in the early 20th century, the overthrow of centralized dictatorship was the same as toppling the rule of the Manchu nobility. As a result, in order to drive the Qing government off the historical stage, there was no better slogan than "National revolution." In 1905, when Sun Zhongshan, the pioneer of China's Bourgeois Revolution (1866–1925), founded the United League (*Tong meng hui*) with various bourgeois political parties, the objective he put forth in the oath was: expelling the Manchus, restoring the Han, founding a republic and equally dividing the land ownership.

Soon, however, these first bourgeois revolutionaries became aware of the following problem in practice: besides the ethnic Han group, China also had a great number of other ethnic groups which had all been living on the territory of the unified country ever since ancient times, also contributing to the creation of China's five-thousand-year-old history and culture. Therefore the question was raised: Is the newly established Republic of China going to include these ethnic groups?

If not, the decision would have been clearly and evidently inconsistent with Chinese history and the unique Chinese cultural tradition that had been in existence for thousands of years.

Liang Qichao (1873–1929), a famous Chinese bourgeoisie thinker, put forth his own doctrine of "nationalism" in earlier times: to fight against the colonial conquest by imperialism, the Chinese people must unite Hans, Manchus, Huis, Miaos, and Tibetans to form one great ethnic group.

In his inaugural address in 1912, Sun Zhongshan, the provisional president of the Republic of China, told the whole world: "The foundation of the country lies in the people; and the unification of lands inhabited by the Han, Manchu,

Mongol, Hui and Tibetan people, into one country, means the unification of the Han, Manchu, Mongol, Hui and Tibetan ethnic groups. It is called national unification." He further pointed out that ethnic groups all belong to this unified Republic of China, meaning one ethnic group should not dominate over another, nor should there be any hostility against Manchu people.

During this period, Tsarist Russia instigated then-Jebtsundamba Khutuktu in Outer Mongolia to declare "independence." At the time, princes of 10 banners, the administrative division of Inner Mongolia Autonomous Region, in Jirem League convened two princely conferences of eastern Mongolia in succession to discuss how to fight Outer Mongolia's "independence." In early 1913, princes of 34 banners in 22 parts of western Mongolia also held a princely conference and decided to team up with eastern Mongolian princes to oppose independence. They issued a telegram statement: "Mongolian territory and the Chinese inland are interdependent, and Hans and Mongolians have been family for centuries. We Mongolians also belong to the Chinese nation, and therefore, should contribute to maintain the unity of the Republic."

It was a solemn political proclamation which shows that even in modern times, when the Western "nation-state" theory was widely spread and put into practice around the world, China's destiny and each ethnic group's choice were still determined by China's unique tradition as well as the mentality formed during its long history and culture.

The Manifesto of the First National Congress of the Kuomintang, issued in 1924, further elaborated China's "nationalism." Kuomintang's nationalism had two meanings: firstly, the Chinese nation seeks liberation independently; and secondly, ethnic groups within China are all equal.

In other words, although Chinese people in modern times

used terms such as "nation" and "nationalism," introduced from the West, they interpreted them based on the reality of Chinese history and culture. Indeed, cultural integrity, solidarity and indivisibility formed over five thousand years are the very components of Chinese history and culture that can not be ignored or transcended. It is also why the Chinese people have had to face their own history and incorporate the modern "nation-state" theory into China's reality when introducing it to the West.

It is intriguing that in the mid-to-late 20th century, the terms "nation" and "nationality" gradually lost their unique designation as a Western modern term in academic, press and publication fields in China, and instead were widely used as a generic term that indicated all concepts concerning "ethnic groups" including "ethnic minorities" both in Chinese history and in reality. For nearly more than half a century, the words "nation" and "nationality," used by Chinese, had nothing to do with the "nation-state" theory implied in Western societies. Only in Western circumstances would Chinese ethnologists consider using the word "nationality" to indicate ethnic groups in ancient China, for example, when writing books in English. Likewise, some organizations related to ethnic minorities also used the word "nationality" when translating their own names.

The reform and opening up starting in the late 1970s has enabled Chinese to better understand Western history and culture. Now many Chinese government agencies, cultural organizations and scholars related to ethnic minorities use the words "nation," "nationality," "ethnic group," or "minority," respectively, in English translation to refer to *minzu*, depending on the context. There are scholars who have made the following suggestions: to use the Chinese nation for *zhonghua minzu*; the ethnic group or the ethnic minorities for the 56 *minzus* in China. It shows that contemporary Chinese people have finally discovered this huge deviation and have adjusted to suit the reality of China.

"Nationalism" in Modern Europe and "Culturalism" in Ancient China

If divergent from the concept of the "nation" in the modern West, then what were the forms and meanings of *minzu* (ethnic group) in ancient China?

Both Chinese historians and Western sinologists have discovered a concept known as "culturalism" in the study of Chinese history. "Culturalism" can be called the nationality of ancient China, in correspondence to "nationalism" in the modern West.

The performance on the Art Festival of Ethnic Minorities.

Professor John King Fairbank (1907–1991), a prominent academic and historian of China in the United States, was also referred to as America's top "China Hand." He once said: "No doubt, the viewpoint that the doctrines of Confucius and Mencius apply to everything implies that Chinese culture (lifestyle) is more fundamental than nationalism… As long as a person is familiar with Confucian classics and behaves accordingly, his skin color or language no longer matters." According to Fairbank, this was how "culturalism" was defined in ancient China.

Ancient China used culture to govern the country and did not divide people by ethnicity. Descent was not the most important criterion to classify ethnic groups, nor was appearance, skin color, or even language. *The Spring and Autumn*

College students from ethnic minorities are watching the flag-raising ceremony on Tiananmen Square.

Annals, the Confucian classic considered to be compiled by Confucius (551–479 BC), wrote: "Vassals are barbarians if adopting barbarian etiquette; barbarians are Chinese if adopting Chinese etiquette." It meant that if vassals adopted barbarian etiquette, they would merely be regarded as barbarians; and if barbarians adopted local etiquette when entering the Central Plain, then they would also be regarded as people of the Central Plain. This was a very liberal door. And its lintel was inscribed with the word etiquette, for example, "the ritual and music culture," a cultural system revolving around values and codes of conduct.

China's territory is geographically special: it is surrounded by natural barriers, and there is a complete system of geographic units inside. Before the Spring and Autumn Period (770–476 BC) and the Warring States Period (475–256 BC), Chinese had formed a distinct national outlook, that is, people believed that being surrounded by seas on all four sides made China the *tianxia* (world)—comprising the Central Plain and *Siyi* (barbarians living in four directions). Therefore, *tianxia* is also referred to as a place "within the four seas."

Generally speaking, *Huaxia* (Hans) living in the Central Plain were considered to be more civilized while people living in the surrounding areas were considered *Siyi* (barbarians living in four directions)—*Dongyi, Nanman, Xirong* and *Beidi*. In the eyes of people of the Central Plain, *Siyi* were significantly different from people of the Central Plain because of their relatively lower level of civilization. During the Xia Dynasty (2070–1600 BC), the Shang Dynasty (1600–1046 BC), and the Western Zhou Dynasty (1046–256 BC), *Huaxia* had already had frequent contacts and exchanges in various ways with *Siyi*. During the Spring and Autumn Period and the Warring States Period, the geographical pattern became more clear—Han people were located in the center (therefore called *Zhongguo,* the Middle Kingdom) with barbarians of *Dongyi, Nanman, Xirong* and *Beidi* in the east, south, west and north, respectively.

In fact, Fairbank insisted that the extent of ethnic differences within China might be even greater than that of all the ethnic differences combined in Europe and America. At the very least, Chinese culture is highly diversified in terms of ethnic groups, ethnic communities, languages and religions, all of which constitute the cultural diversity of China. With such great cultural diversity, how has China been able to maintain its unity for thousands of years?

Ancient Chinese had an unparalleled admiration for "the ritual and music culture," and were also optimistic about its spreading and its mutual understanding among communities. They claimed: "Chinese will degrade into barbarians if evil, and barbarians will upgrade into Chinese if virtuous." The standard did not only apply to *Siyi,* but also to people of the Central Plain who were in a privileged position. Therefore, the door that divided different groups of people was not eternally open or closed—it was flexible, providing free access. When *Siyi* entered the door, they became *Huaxia;* by the same token, *Huaxia* was not an unchangeable tag either, because when *Huaxia* stepped out the door, they became *Siyi.*

The debate over *Huaxia* and *Siyi* did not rely on ethnicity but on the level of civilization a society had achieved. There was always a greater flexibility and dialectics behind the sense of privilege felt by people of the Central Plain over barbarians. That is, people of the Central Plain believed that barbarians could become civilized people through "enlightenment." Based on the ethnic-community viewpoint that "everyone is entitled to be educated," Chinese cultural tradition held: the mission of the Kingdom in the Central Plain was to turn barbarians into "people of the Celestial Empire" through enlightenment rather than military force—so as to achieve "Great Harmony."

As a matter of fact, the system of enlightenment by "the ritual and music culture" was not created solely by *Huaxia* communities in the Central Plain, but was rather an outcome of communication and integration between people from different areas. For example, the emperors of the Shang Dynasty were from *Dongyi*, the emperors of the Zhou Dynasty were from western areas, and even *Huaxia* people in the Central Plain themselves had originated from pioneer communities, but had overtime made progress in history through communication and integration. This is why the fundamental concept in ancient Chinese culture states: "There are *Siyi* in *Huaxia* people and there are also *Huaxia* in *Siyi* people." Based on this notion, a consensus took form deep within Chinese culture and tradition: people around the world are all equal in terms of origin.

In this way, the standards, which allowed alteration in different contexts, left great historical possibility with *Siyi*. Just was owing to the impact of this "culturalism." When *Siyi* had the opportunity to enter the Central Plain, their motive was not to occupy the land and destroy Central Plain culture. On the contrary, their biggest hope was to become the orthodox of "the ritual and music culture" of the Central Plain themselves. Therefore, "culturalism" became a highly inclusive historical container, making Central Plain culture a historical heritage to be inherited and passed down instead of open to attack by later dynastic changes.

Compared with other ancient civilizations in the world, this sense of "culturalism" can be viewed as flexible and unique to Chinese culture. Its ability to open and close passageways arguably makes it is more dynamic and inclusive than other forms of "culturalism," while at the same time, allowing for the possibility of achieving integrity, solidarity and indivisibility in Chinese culture.

Chinese offer "culturalism" as one explanation to Westerners who cannot understand why Chinese civilization has been able to develop uninterrupted for five thousand years. It also serves to help explain why China has been able to maintain a unified multiethnic country for over two thousand years.

The Pattern of Diversity
in Unity of the Chinese Nation

Ethnic Identification: How Many Ethnic Groups Are There in China?

The People's Republic of China was founded on October 1, 1949 and the first visiting delegation to ethnic regions sent by the central government started in June of 1950—shortly after the founding of New China. Taking into account the fact that voluminous complex matters were waiting ahead for the newly established country to deal with, it can be argued that ethnic minority affairs were considered a top priority for this country.

From 1950 to 1953, the Chinese government sent four delegations in succession to ethnic minority regions in the southwest, northwest, central south and northeast. These large-scale delegations had long journeys before them; the delegation to the southwest, with as many as 120 members, traveled to Sichuan, Yunnan and Guizhou provinces for as long as seven months. The delegation's mission was

Autumn scenery in Altay region of northern Xijiang. The population of ethnic minorities in Xinjiang accounts for nearly 60% of the total local population.

to inform ethnic minorities around the country of the new government's basic policies: the People's Republic of China will achieve full equality among all ethnic groups within its territory, respect religious beliefs and folklore customs of all ethnic groups, and develop the economy and culture of ethnic minorities vigorously.

A Tibetan compact community on Tibetan Plateau.

Equality among ethnic groups is a cornerstone of China's ethnic policy. In China, the definition of full equality among ethnic groups includes three aspects: first, regardless of their population size, length of history, area of residence, level of economic development, differences in spoken and written languages, religious beliefs, folkways and customs, every ethnic group has equal political status; second, all ethnic groups in China have not only political and legal equality, but also economic, cultural and social equality; third, citizens of all ethnic groups are equal before the law, enjoying the same rights and performing the same duties.

New ethnic policies have encouraged self-acknowledgement of ethnic groups and active expression of their own ethnic wishes and rights. This can be seen from the result of the first census in 1953—more than 400 ethnic group names were registered, with over 260 names in Yunnan Province alone.

Among these 400 names, some used different names for the same ethnic group, some were the names of different branches of an ethnic group, some were ethnic group names based on residence, and some were even different Chinese transliterations of the same name of an ethnic group. This prompted a closer examination of ethnic groups in China, and immediately the task of ethnic identification was set.

Many renowned ethnologists and sociologists in China traveled to several communities, where people were waiting to confirm their ethnic identities. A great number of historians and linguists also participated in the event which was particularly important for the country.

The process of ethnic identification proved to be a very arduous one. It took over twenty years from 1953, when the State Ethnic Affairs Commission dispatched the first investigative team, to 1979, when the Jino ethnic group was the last one to be identified. Considering the length of time, the amount of manpower the Chinese government has spent and the scale of the work, scholars agree in unison with the following statement made years later: The ethnic identification in the 20th century is the largest and an unprecedented one in Chinese history; it is pioneering work for China—and it is seldom seen in the world.

There are three goals for ethnic identification: to identify whether a community belongs to the Han ethnic group or to the ethnic minorities; to identify whether this ethnic community is a separate ethnic group or part of another ethnic minority; and to confirm the ethnic identity and the name of the ethnic community.

In 1953, the identification team for the She minority in Zhejiang and Fujian provinces was the first investigative agency that had been set up to identify ethnic groups. Shi Lianzhu, the principal of the team, later became the most famous scholar in the study of the She minority and wrote *The Ethnic Identification in China*.

Most ethnic communities that were identified were situated in areas where transportation was inconvenient, leaving investigators to climb mountains and cross rivers on foot. The She minority that Shi and his team were trying to identify had been regarded as part of the Han ethnic group, or a branch of the Yao minority. After the investigation, however, it was found to be a separate ethnic minority.

What were the criteria of ethnic identification in China? Iosif Vissarionovich Stalin (1897–1953) offered a simple and clear definition of "ethnic groups" in his book *Marxism and the National Question*: "A nation is a historically constituted, stable community of people, formed on the basis of a common language, territory, economic life, and psychological make-up manifested in a common culture." This passage provided great inspiration for people working on ethnic affairs in China at the time. Although this definition was put forth for nationalities in the modern West, Chinese ethnologists thought it had a universal significance. Therefore a common language, territory, economic life and psychological make-up became four major criteria for ethnic identification in China.

Nevertheless, China's national circumstance at the time must be taken into account. China's ethnic identification incorporated the actual situations of its ethnic minorities, and apart from Stalin's definition, "ethnic willingness," "historical basis," and "proximity identification" became three important principles.

"Ethnic willingness" meant that ethnic identities and names could not be imposed; identifiers and governments could not decide ethnic identities for people; people to be identified could actively make their ethnic wishes heard and have the right to fully negotiate with the government.

"Historical basis" meant that apart from field investigation into an ethnic group's real life, cultural heritages such as voluminous documents, old scriptures, records and stone tablets as well as mythologies and songs, must be fully used.

"Proximity identification" expressed the following idea: similar ethnic communities, for example, adjacent ethnic communities that basically had the same language, close economic ties, and mutual acknowledgement, should be combined and identified as one ethnic group, so long as this was beneficial to the ethnic groups' own development.

During the decade after 1953, ethnic identification gradually entered its climax.

Of all regions, ethnic identification in Yunnan Province

was the most difficult. In 1954, the State Ethnic Affair Commission sent an ethnic identification team to Yunnan Province. Linguists played a pivotal role in the identification process. The phonological system and grammatical structure of language served as a measurable and objective basis for ethnic identification. Over 3 million people in Yunnan Province spoke the Yi language but used tens of different names for their ethnicity. They were, however, all identified as branches of the Yi minority rather than a separate one, based on the fact that they shared common linguistic characteristics and, of course, common cultural traditions such as the Torch Festival, the Native Chieftain System; the practice that marriage between people bearing the same surname was forbidden, as well as cremation sites, ancestor posts, witchcraft and so on. At last, over 260 different ethnic communities in Yunnan Province were identified as 22 ethnic groups.

The identification of the Tujia minority was particularly

A local village of the Dong minority in Guizhou which is home to numerous ethnic minorities.

Terraced paddy fields of the Hani minority in Yuanyang, Yunnan Province.

tortuous. The Tujia minority which had no written language of their own but spoke Mandarin prevalently sparked a great academic controversy in its identification as a separate ethnic group. Pan Guangdan (1899–1967), a main figure in this process, firmly believed that the Tujia minority did not belong to the Miao or Yao minorities in the area and that it was a dependent ethnic minority originating from ancient Ba people. Pan suffered from severe myopia, but he made more than 1,300 notes related to the Tujia minority and ancient Ba people. Even with a bad leg, he travelled across the vast lands of the Tu minority on crutches. Finally, the Tujia minority was officially acknowledged as a single ethnic group at last.

By the start of the Cultural Revolution in 1966, the last ethnic minority that had been identified was the Lhoba minority living in Shannan and Linzhi regions in Tibet. Until then, 54 ethnic minorities had been identified in China, leaving only a few ethnic communities unidentified.

During the Cultural Revolution, ethnic identification was forced to a halt. In 1978, when the opening up and reform began, ethnic identification was picked up where it was left off. In Yunnan Province, an ethnologist named Du Yuting took on the academic debate from over a decade ago: were the Jino people inhabiting collectively on Jino Mountain in Jinghong County, Yunnan Province truly a branch of the Yi minority? Du returned to Jino Mountain and began to look for more evidence, conducting further research. That same year, a research group consisting of thirty to forty people including historians, linguists and ethnologists also went to Jino Mountain. The result of their collective study was that the Jino people were indeed a single ethnic minority.

On June 6, 1979, the Jino minority of just over twenty thousand people officially became the last ethnic minority identified in China during the 20th century.

O Data Link

Fifty-five Ethnic Minorities in China

Ethnicity	Main Residence Regions	Population (people)
The Mongol minority	Inner-Mongolia, Liaoning, Jilin, Hebei, Heilongjiang, Xinjiang	5,813,947
The Hui minority	Ningxia, Gansu, Henan, Xinjiang, Qinghai, Yunnan, Hebei Shandong, Anhui, Liaoning, Beijing, Inner-Mongolia, Tianjin, Heilongjiang, Shaanxi, Guizhou, Jilin, Jiangsu, Sichuan	9,816,805
The Tibetan minority	Tibet, Sichuan, Qinghai, Gansu, Yunnan	5,416,021
The Uygur minority	Xinjiang	8,399,393
The Miao minority	Guizhou, Hunan, Yunnan, Guangxi, Chongqing, Hubei, Sichuan	8,940,116
The Yi minority	Yunnan, Sichuan, Guizhou	7,762,272
The Zhuang minority	Guangxi, Yunnan, Guangdong	16,178,811
The Bouyei minority	Guizhou	2,971,460
The Korean minority	Jilin, Heilongjiang, Liaoning	1,923,842
The Manchu minority	Liaoning, Hebei, Heilongjiang, Jilin, Inner Mongolia, Beijing	10,682,262
The Dong minority	Guizhou, Hunan, Guangxi	2,960,293
The Yao minority	Guangxi, Hunan, Yunnan, Guangdong	2,637,421
The Bai minority	Yunnan, Guizhou, Hunan	1,858,063
The Tujia minority	Hunan, Hubei, Chongqing, Guizhou	8,028,133
The Hani minority	Yunnan	1,439,673
The Kazak minority	Xinjiang	1,250,458
The Dai minority	Yunnan	1,158,989
The Li minority	Hainan	1,247,814
The Lisu minority	Yunnan, Sichuan	634,912
The Va minority	Yunnan	396,610
The She minority	Fujian, Zhejiang, Jiangxi, Guangdong	709,592
The Gaoshan minority	Taiwan, Fujian	4,461
The Lahu minority	Yunnan	453,705
The Sui minority	Guizhou, Guangxi	406,902
The Dongxiang minority	Gansu, Xinjiang	513,805

Ethnicity	Main Residence Regions	Population (people)
The Naxi minority	Yunnan	308,839
The Jingpo minority	Yunnan	132,143
The Kirgiz minority	Xinjiang	160,823
The Tu minority	Qinghai, Gansu	241,198
The Daur minority	Inner-Mongolia, Heilongjiang	132,394
The Mulam minority	Guangxi	207,352
The Qiang minority	Sichuan	306,072
The Blang minority	Yunnan	91,882
The Salar minority	Qinghai	104,503
The Maonan minority	Guangxi	107,166
The Gelao minority	Guizhou	579,357
The Xibe minorit	Liaoning, Xinjiang	188,824
The Achang minority	Yunnan	33,936
The Pumi minority	Yunnan	33,600
The Tajik minority	Xinjiang	41,028
The Nu minority	Yunnan	28,759
The Ozbek minority	Xinjiang	12,370
The Russian minority	Xinjiang, Heilongjiang	15,609
The Ewenki minority	Inner Mongolia	30,505
The De'ang minority	Yunnan	17,935
The Bonan minority	Gansu	16,505
The Yugur minority	Gansu	13,719
The Jing minority	Guangxi	22,517
The Tatar minority	Xinjiang	4,890
The Derung minority	Yunnan	7,426
The Oroqen minority	Heilongjiang, Inner Mongolia	8,196
The Hezhen minority	Heilongjiang	4,640
The Monba minority	Tibet	8,923
The Lhoba minority	Tibet	2,965
The Jino minority	Yunnan	20,899

*Population data taken from the 2000 Census.
*The population of the Gaoshan minority does not include Taiwan Province.

Thus far, 55 ethnic minorities had been officially identified in China. In effect, there still remain a few ethnic communities that are waiting to be identified in China, and therefore, this work has yet to completely end.

The Pattern of Diversity in Unity of the Chinese Nation

Neither visiting delegations to ethnic regions, shortly after the establishment of the PRC, nor ethnic identification starting from 1953, had made the Chinese government believe its understanding of ethnic minorities was sufficient. In 1956, a larger scale investigation on ethnic minority societies and histories began around the country.

This investigation was proposed by Chairman Mao Zedong (1893–1976), and was implemented by the NPC's Ethnic Affairs Committee. The investigation organizer's plan was in the following four to seven years obtain a clearer picture of the situations of major ethnic minorities in China.

More than 1,000 scholars took part in this massive undertaking. According to incomplete statistics, the investigation comprised: over 340 investigative materials which included written works with a total of 29 million words—of which 15 million words were derived from a collection of over 100 archives and excerpts—and over 10 documentaries. By 1966, the scholars involved in the investigation submitted primary research findings on China's ethnic minorities, which resulted in 57 rough manuscripts titled *Concise History*, *Brief Records* and *History & Brief Records*.

This was a crucial event for Chinese in attaining a sensible understanding of ethnic minorities of China.

Fei Xiaotong (1910–2005) was the major organizer and participant of the investigation on ethnic minority societies and histories. Furthermore, he was also a steady hand in a

series of important historical events related to ethnic minorities in the 1950s—and was a part of many of the visiting delegations that traveled to several ethnic minority regions. It was after his close contacts with ethnic minorities that several crucial historical questions began circling in the back of his mind: in China, how had the societies and histories of the Han ethnic group and ethnic minorities impacted each other? What were ethnic minorities' effects upon the formation of the ethnic Han group? How should the "Chinese nation" which includes the ethnic Han group and 55 other ethnic minorities be understood?

Tomb of Genghis Khan in Inner-Mongolia, the holy place for the Mongol minority to pay tribute to their ancestor Genghis Khan.

He dwelt on these questions for as long as 30 years. In 1989, Fei first lectured about his work *Pattern of Diversity in Unity of the Chinese Nation* at the Chinese University of Hong Kong.

His work met immediately with strong academic attention. After many intense academic debates, his ideas were gradually improved upon, and they have since become the basis of a mainstream theory explaining the origin, formation and development of the Chinese nation.

Fei's *Pattern of Diversity in Unity of the Chinese Nation* is regarded as the theory which explains the formation of the Chinese nation, including its 55 ethnic minorities. It states that: "The Chinese nation's mainstream is a pattern of diversity in unity, which was formed by communicating, mixing, allaying and integratiing as well as splitting and declining; that all components are interacting and integrating with each other, but also maintain their own characteristics." About the formation process its writes: "As early as 3,000 years ago, a core community, called *Huaxia*, formed by several ethnic groups' converging and integrating, came into being in the middle reaches of the Yellow River and started to snowball and affiliate other surrounding ethnic groups. When they occupied the plains in the middle and lower reaches of the Yangzi River and Yellow River in East Asia, they were called the Han ethnic group by others. The Han ethnic group absorbed parts of other ethnic groups and enlarged itself continuously. It also penetrated into other ethnic groups' compact communities and formed a network that played a uniting and connecting role. It laid the foundation for an indivisible united community consisting of many ethnic groups in this region, became an ethnic entity, and called itself the Chinese nation when it became self-aware."

The *Huaxia* ethnic community—the precursor to the Han ethnic group—had diverse origins. It began with the collision and integration of different cultures in the middle and lower reaches of the Yellow River. In the Western Zhou Dynasty, cultures in varying regions still maintained their own characteristics. However, due to massive population fluxes and regional shifts which occurred during the five hundred years of the Spring and Autumn Period and the Warring

States Period, several cultures were forced to engage and interact with one another, driving Chinese history into its first climax when the Han ethnic group began maturing into an ethnic entity.

The term "Han" became an ethnic group name at the initial stage of the Southern and Northern Dynasties (420–589). A great number of nomadic peoples such *Xianbei, Hun, Di, Qiang,* and *Jie* entered the Central Plain one after another in the 4th and 5th century when Han people and non-Han vassals were communicating and integrating. Thus, "Han" became known as the original residents of the Central Plain. During the Southern and Northern Dynasties, ethnic groups were living among one another and interacting. It was during this dynamic period when diverse Han ethnic communities gradually became unified. By the end of the era,

The Potala Palace in the center of Lhasa, symbol of Tibetan history and culture.

these nomadic peoples travelling in the Central Plain all integrated themselves into one ethnic group which eventually became known as "Han." Their own ethnic group names disappeared one by one; their cultures were taken in by the Han culture and also became part of it. This appeared to be the result of intermarriages, which were very common at the time between ethnic groups that were living in the same area. The development of the Han during this period is further historically significant as it also gave rise to China's traditional "culturalism."

The split of the Southern and Northern Dynasties ended in the unification during the Sui (581–618) and Tang (618–907) dynasties. The ruling classes in both dynasties had non-Han origins themselves. The royal court of the Sui Dynasty was full of *Xianbei* statesmen, and even King Wen of Sui Dynasty himself, the founder of the dynasty, married a *Xianbei*. The following Tang Dynasty inherited this practice and Li Yuan (618–626), the founder of the Tang Dynasty, was born to a *Xianbei* mother and married a *Xianbei* as his queen. Early in the Tang Dynasty, *Xianbei* nobles willing to be converted by the Han culture played a pivotal role and were serving in important positions from the very beginning. In other words, the Tang Dynasty that Chinese are so proud of is actually one great dynasty that was created by many ethnic groups altogether. Though it was ruled by the Han ethnic group in name, all ethnic groups had in fact participated in the administration.

Ethnic group names such *Xianbei*, *Di* and *Jie* disappeared in the long river of history with the end of the Sui and Tang dynasties—as for nearly 500 years from the Southern and Northern Dynasties to the Tang Dynasty, the Central Plain was in reality a melting pot of ethnic groups, with the Han ethnic group serving as the core.

The following Northern Song (960–1127) and Southern

Song (1127–1279) dynasties continued to interact actively with emerging nomadic peoples in the north. The *Qidan* ethnic group set up a strong Liao Kingdom, but when the name *Qidan* spread to Europe as a byword of China, the *Qidan* ethnic group itself had already disappeared on the lands of the Central Plain. The bulk of the *Qidan* ethnic group had been conquered and destroyed by other northern nomadic people called *Nvzhen*, leaving the remaining Qidan minority to gradually become members of the "Han" people. The *Dangxiang* people, who established the Xixia Kingdom to the northwest of the Northern Song Dynasty, also vanished after a two-hundred-year-long era of prosperity when they were devastated by Mongolian military forces. Again, those remaining *Dangxiang* people later peacefully integrated themselves into the "Han" people.

The historical evolution of Chinese shows that the Han ethnic group is by no means an ethnic group with only one origin. At the same time, during all periods in Chinese history, there were always trends moving in the opposite direction, too. In other regions, Han also fused with other ethnic groups.

Many Han people moved to border barbarian areas due to factors such as wars, natural disasters and military settlement. For example, the war at the end of the Eastern Han Dynasty prompted more than a hundred thousand households to flee to areas where the *Wuhuan* ethnic group lived. These Han people who had moved to border ethnic regions had to change their lifestyle and folklore in order to adapt to the new local environments and social life surrounding them, and subsequently they became a part of local ethnic groups.

The *Gaochang* Kingdom set up by the *Qus* in Turfan, Xinjiang in AD 499 was originally a state consisting mostly of settled soldiers in the Han-Wei period and fleeing Han people in the Jin Dynasty, but it discarded Han people's dressing and linguistic traditions. In the end, it was assimilated into the Uygur minority.

Such a phenomenon was very common. The Han people that migrated into Yunnan Province during the thousands of years before the Ming Dynasty also mostly integrated into local ethnic groups. The *Bai* ethnic group is another example of yet another ethnic group that incorporated people of Han origins.

As for the formation of the Tibetan minority, Gelek Lobsang, the first Tibetan scholar who has earned a PhD in China, drew the following conclusion based on his long-term study: "The ancient Tibetan culture does not fall from the sky, but instead it was formed on the basis of the original culture in the southern valley of Tibet, by absorbing and integrating the primitive nomadic culture in northern grassland and nomadic peoples belonging to the Hu ethnic strain as well as Yangshao culture in the Central Plain and ethnic groups belonging to the Di and Qiang ethnic strains."

Speaking further on the subject, Fei's *Pattern of Diversity in Unity of the Chinese Nation* wrote: "Speaking from the viewpoint of biological basis, or so-called "lineage," mixing and blending often occur in the "unity" of the Chinese nation, as it were, so there is not a single ethnic group that is "pure-blood" in terms of lineage."

Diversity and unity are two indivisible and interdependent trends that ethnic groups in China have demonstrated over its long history. After the Opium War in 1840, in the fight against the invasion of Western imperialism and Japanese militarism, people from all ethnic groups formed a self-conscious ethnic entity, which would later prove to stand together through times of thick and thin.

Thus, the pattern of diversity in unity of the Chinese nation, formed in this way, has the following aspects, according to Fei's *Pattern of Diversity in Unity of the Chinese Nation*:

"First, the Chinese nation is an ethnic entity that includes 56 ethnic groups in China, rather than a generic name for 56 ethnic groups simply added together. Fifty-six ethnic groups

● Data Link

The Pattern of "Great Unity" in Ancient China

As early as in the pre-Qin Dynasty times before 221 BC, the concepts of "country" and "unification" had taken shape in the minds of Chinese people. In 221 BC, the Qin Dynasty unified the country for the first time. It put the regions, including today's Guangxi Zhuang Autonomous Region and Yunnan Province, where minority peoples were concentrated, under its jurisdiction. The subsequent Han Dynasty (206 BC–220 AD) further consolidated the country's unification. It set up the Protectorate of the Western Regions in today's Xinjiang Uygur Autonomous Region, and added 17 prefectures to govern the people of all ethnic groups. The Qin and Han dynasties created the fundamental framework of China as a unified multiethnic country.

The Tang Dynasty (618–907) established the Anxi Protector-general's Office and Beiting Protector-general's Office to manage administrative affairs in the Western Regions, including today's Xinjiang, and set up *Dao*, *Fu* and *Zhou* (equivalent to today's province, prefecture and county) to administer minority peoples in south central and southwestern China. The Yuan Dynasty (1206–1368), established by the Mongols, appointed aboriginal officials or *tuguan* (hereditary posts of local administrators filled by chiefs of ethnic minorities) in the *Fu* and *Zhou* of the southern regions where minority peoples lived in compact communities. The central government set up the Commission for Buddhist and Tibetan Affairs under it, whereby Tibet was thenceforth brought under the effective administration of the central government of China. The Yuan also founded the Penghu Military Inspectorate for the administration of the Penghu Islands and Taiwan. Most of modern China's ethnic groups were subjects of the Yuan Dynasty. The Qing Dynasty (1644–1911), founded by the Manchus, set up the Ili Generalship and Xinjiang Province in the Western Regions, appointed Grand Minister Resident in Tibet and established the system of conferring honorific titles on two Living Buddhas—the Dalai and Panchen—by the central government. In addition, the Qing court carried out a series of political reforms in southwestern China, including the policy of gaituguiliu, for example, appropriating the governing power of local hereditary aboriginal chieftains and setting up the system of appointment of local administrators by the central government in the minority areas. China's territory in the Qing Dynasty was basically the same as that of today.

have already formed an interdependent and indivisible unity, in which all components have already obtained a higher level ethnic recognition, for example, to share weal and woe, to live or die together, to share glory and shame, and to share a common destiny. Second, the pattern of diversity in unity must go through a process when scattered components gradually unite together. There needs to be a core that plays a uniting role. The Han ethnic group is one of many basic components that has united all components, but this unity was no longer the Han ethnic group but the Chinese nation—an ethnic group of higher recognition. Third, high-level recognition does not necessarily replace or reject lower level recognition. Different levels can coexist, even make a good use of their own original strengths based on this pattern, and form a unity of multiple languages and cultures."

The Overall Situation of Ethnic Minority Populations in China

The Ethnic Minority Population in China

In terms of population, China has the world's largest population by country, with its Han ethnic group ranking the largest of ethnic groups in the world (according to a 2000 census, there were 1.159 billion Han people in mainland China). There are also other impressive population figures within China: the Zhuang minority, the most populous ethnic minority in China, has a population of 16.18 million, equal to that of a medium-sized country in Europe; meanwhile the Lhoba minority, the least populous ethnic group in China, has a mere population of 2,965–5,550 times smaller than the Zhuang ethnic group.

It is almost impossible to find another country in the world with such impressive showings in population.

Since the establishment of the PRC, the government has carried out a series of five large-scale censuses around the country. The first was in 1953, and it ascertained that the ethnic minority population was 34.0138 million. This was the first time such a task had been completed in China's thousands of years of history. None of the previous dynasties had completed any statistics regarding ethnic minority popula-

Girls of the Zhuang minority. The Zhuang minority is the largest ethnic minority, mainly concentrating in Guangxi Zhuang Autonomous Region.

tions. Therefore, until this census, the populations of ethnic minorities had long been a "big mystery."

The most recent census, which ended in 2000, was also the largest one in Chinese history. Its results show that the total population of China's ethnic minorities had reached 106.43 million. This means that from 1953 to 2000, the ethnic minority population in China had increased by 2.07 times.

During the same period, the total population for mainland China had increased by 1.15 times; while the population of the Han ethnic group in mainland China had increased by 1.10 times.

The results show that during about fifty years between the first and the fifth census, the growth rate of China's ethnic minority population is much bigger than that of the total population on average and that of the Han ethnic group population on average.

The result of the fifth census also shows that ethnic minority populations account for 8.41 percent of the total population in mainland China. In the third census in 1982, ethnic minority populations accounted for 6.62 percent of the total population in mainland China; and in the fourth census in 1990, 8.01 percent. This means that the proportion of ethnic

A young man of the Lhoba minority. The Lhoba minority is the least populated ethnic group of China, mainly inhabiting the southeast of Tibet.

The elderly of the Hui minority. The Hui minority is an ethnic group with the widest distribution in China, and Ningxia Hui Autonomous Region is the largest region inhabited by the Hui people in compact communities.

Ethnic Groups and Religions in China

minorities among the country's total population is rising year after year.

In addition, the 2000 census also disclosed some other significant details:

Among 55 ethnic minorities, the number of ethnic groups whose populations are bigger than 10 million has increased from the Zhuang minority, to the Zhuang and Manchu minorities; while the Hui, Miao and Uygur minorities are quickly approaching this number.

The number of ethnic groups whose populations are bigger than 1 million has increased from 10 groups in 1953, to 18 groups in 2000.

There are 20 ethnic groups whose populations are smaller than 50,000, among which 8 groups have populations smaller than 10,000.

While the populations of most ethnic minorities are rising, their growth rates differ from one to another.

As many as 38 ethnic groups have a fast-growing or an

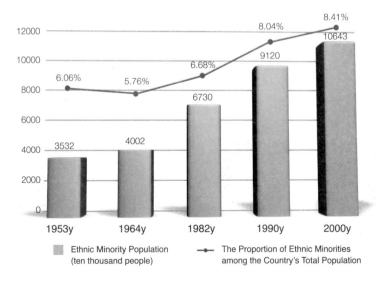

The Proportion of Ethnic Minorities in Five Censuses

Ethnic Minority Population (ten thousand people)

The Proportion of Ethnic Minorities among the Country's Total Population

1953y — 3532 — 6.06%
1964y — 4002 — 5.76%
1982y — 6730 — 6.68%
1990y — 9120 — 8.04%
2000y — 10643 — 8.41%

extremely fast-growing population, including the Gelao minority (8.80 percent), the Tujia minority (7.78 percent), the Jing minority (4.66 percent), the Xibo minority (4.96 percent), the Qiang minority (4.64 percent), the Hezhen ethnic group (5.26 percent), the Lhoba minority (5.72 percent), and the Maonan minority (4.40 percent).

Eleven ethnic group populations are growing relatively fast, including the Tibetan, Uygur and Yi minorities whose populations are larger than 1 million.

The population of the Korean minority is growing relatively slow.

Meanwhile, three ethnic groups that have seen their populations decrease: the Russian (-7.83 percent), Ozbek (-0.20 percent), and Tartar (-0.73 percent) minorities.

Population Policies towards Ethnic Minorities in China

China's population policies towards ethnic minorities are made in accordance with practices adopted by ethnic minority populations from different periods, social and economic development in ethnic regions and the wishes of ethnic minorities.

Since 1950, population policies towards ethnic minorities have gone through three phases:

I. Encouraging population policies (1950–1970).

Policies in this period were made according to two main factors: first, at the beginning of the PRC, natural growth rates of some ethnic minority populations were low, and some groups even saw their populations decreasing. They were on the verge of fading out as their populations continued to drop; second, most ethnic minorities were still using a traditional economic model in which social development relied directly on the increase of laborers.

Based on these points, the Chinese government employed a policy aimed at boosting these populations.

During the first half of the 20th century, populations of some ethnic minorities continued to drop severely. According to statistics, up until 1951, when serfdom was still in place in Tibet, the death rate was as high as 28 per thousand and the infant mortality rate as high as 430 per thousand—that is to say, nearly half of every 1,000 infants died at birth, or shortly thereafter.

Hunters of the Oroqen minority. The Oroqen minority is mainly distributed in Inner-Mongolia and Heilongjiang Province etc.

The Oroqen minority is an ethnic group living in northeast China. Reportedly, its population in 1917 was around 4,000 people, about 3,000 in 1938, and only 2,256 by 1953. Over the last 36 years, its population had decreased by 45.12 percent. Such slumps were rarely seen in history.

The government's population policy yielded positive results soon after its implementation. In 1953, ethnic minority populations stopped dropping and began to grow slowly. Then by the mid-1960s, ethnic minority populations started to increase rapidly. According to statistics, China's ethnic minority population increased from 34 million in 1953 to 39 million in 1964.

The population of the Oroqen minority also increased steadily. By 1990, its population reached 6,965 people, and by 2000, this number had already climbed to 8,196.

II. The family planning policy in-the-making (1971–1981).

In the 1970s, the Chinese government began to carry out the family planning policy in regions where the Han ethnic group was living, encouraging couples to have only one child. But for ethnic minorities, the government had always adopted the policy of "ethnic minority regions exempted." In other words, this policy only applied to the Han ethnic group.

During this period, the government continued to encourage population growth of ethnic minorities. By 1980, the fertility rate of ethnic minority women was 4.49, or 69.43 percent higher than that of the Han ethnic group (2.65). From 1964 to 1982, the total ethnic minority population saw a net increase of 26 million, accounting for 78.06 percent of the total population of ethnic minorities in 1953.

Herdsmen of the Mongol minority.

III. Flexible family planning policy (1982–present)

Population policies towards ethnic minorities in this period are made based on the fact that population of ethnic minorities are exploding and bringing about a series of challenges. In some regions, the overpopulation of ethnic minorities has hindered economic development. The National Family Planning Commission has sent scholars to ethnic regions such as Guangxi and Yunnan for field tours several

The Uygur folk
entertainment
"Maxrap."

times and noted that the baby boom in these areas is causing problems to living standards; in order to meet the demand of bigger populations, some ethnic minorities have had to cut down trees and reclaim wasteland, leading to various ecological disasters such as severe water loss, soil erosion, growing desertification and petrifaction.

The difficulties arising in such population growth has triggered a debate: should ethnic minorities carry out the family planning policy?

Meanwhile, the Han ethnic regions have reached a consensus over the family planning policy. As such the phrase: "have fewer children, get rich faster" has become a popular sentiment among them. This has convinced some government officials and scholars from ethnic minorities to call in favor of the implementation of the family planning policy for ethnic minorities. At the same time, however, there is a countering viewpoint that population growth should be encouraged to make up for the shortage of labor in China, since ethnic minority populations are still much smaller than that of the Han ethnic group, and compact communities of ethnic minorities are sparsely populated.

The Chinese have attached great importance to both viewpoints. The new ethnic minority population policy has fully considered the concrete situations of ethnic minorities against different demographic backdrops in different regions, with its guiding principle as follows: the wishes of ethnic minorities should be respected and policies should be made according to local conditions; the governments of ethnic autonomous regions have the right to decide whether or not, when, and how to implement the family planning policy among local ethnic minorities.

Therefore, the family planning policy has been gradually implemented in ethnic regions. It was carried out in Ningxia Hui Autonomous Region in 1984; and in Xinjiang Uygur Autonomous Region and Inner Mongolia Autonomous Region in 1988.

Women of the Gaoshan minority. The Gaoshan minority inhabits Taiwan Province of China. Of a total population of 400,000, over 4000 people are living in the mainland of China.

Ningxia Hui Autonomous Region provides that: workers, urban residents and farmers are allowed to have two children if the husband and wife are both, or one of them is, from an ethnic minoritiy. Ethnic minority farmers living in mountainous areas are allowed to have three children.

Guangxi Zhuang Autonomous Region provides that: if both the husband and wife are from ethnic minorities whose populations are smaller than 10 million, they are allowed to have two children.

Xinjiang Uygur Autonomous Region provides that: for urban residents from ethnic minorities, couples are allowed to have two children; for herdsmen and farmers from ethnic minorities, couple are allowed to have three children or four children, if they meet certain requirements; for people from ethnic minorities that have a population of less than 50,000, couples are allowed to have four children.

Inner Mongolia Autonomous Region stipulates: for the Mongol minority, couples are allowed to have two children; non-urban Mongolian couples are allowed to have three children; and no restrictions shall be placed upon ethnic minorities with extremely low populations such as the Daur, Ewenki and Oroqen minorities; for other ethnic minorities, couples are allowed to have two children.

Yunnan, Guizhou and Qinghai provinces respectively provide: that ethnic minority couples can have two children; for ethnic minorities under special circumstances, farmers and herdsmen can have three children following government approval; the family planning policy does not apply to ethnic minorities with populations lower than 100,000. There is no quota for births, either.

Tibet is an exception. Since the vast land of Tibet is sparsely populated, the family planning policy only applies to government officials, workers and urban residents who account for 12 percent of the total population of the entire region; it does not apply to Tibetans in rural and pastoral areas who account for 88 percent of the total population in this region. There is no quota for births. This policy has remained unchanged from 1982 to the present.

Some Demographic Indicators of Ethnic Minorities Catching up and Nearing the Level of the Han Ethnic Group

In December 1989, Zhang Tianlu published his book *Ethnic Minority Demography*. It was at this time that the ethinc minority demography was born as a discipline in China.

The fourth census in 1990 provided a precious research opportunity for the new discipline. Zhang analyzed the results of the census immediately, and drew some important conclusions.

Zhang's research made during this period on "ethnic minorities are catching up and nearing the level of the Han ethnic group in terms of demographic indicators" has

Fishermen of the Jing minority living near the Northern Gulf in Guangxi Province. The Jing minority is the only coastal settler among all the ethnic minorities in China.

drawn great media attention. This research is based on the following premise: in history, China's ethnic minorities generally or significantly lagged behind the Han ethnic group in terms of culture, economy, et cetera. It has long been a common view that ethnic minorities lag behind the Han ethnic group; after the establishment of the PRC, the government proposed that ethnic minorities should catch up and move closer to the Han ethnic group in all aspects. This viewpoint then begs the question: can ethnic minorities catch up with the Han ethnic group—and when?

From the 1990 census, Zhang made a detailed analysis and drew the following conclusions:

By 1990, a total of 26 ethnic minorities had surpassed the Han ethnic group in one or more of 22 indicators such as natural population growth, women's fertility rate, infant mortality, average life expectancy, adult illiteracy rate, overall average education level, urbanization level, the tertiary industry and quality of life, respectively. Among them, the Korean minority surpassed the Han ethnic group in 20 demographic indicators;

A girl of the Korean minority. The Korean minority is mainly distributed in Heilongjiang, Jinlin and Liaoning provinces.

the Manchu minority in 18; the Xibe minority in 14, and the Russian minority in 13; both the Gaoshan and Ozbek minorities in 10; 9 for the Daur minority; 8 for the Mongol, Tatar, Hezhen, Yugur and Ewenki minorities; 7 for the Jing and Hui minorities; 5 for the Kazak minority; 4 for both the Tujia and Mulam minorities; 3 for the Maonan minority; 2 for the Zhuang and She minorities; 1 for the Tibetan, Hani, Naxi, Gelao and Bouyei minorities.

Zhang's conclusions have punctured a persistent traditional viewpoint in Chinese society: ethnic minorities always lag behind the Han ethnic group. With these objective demographic indicators, he passed an irresistible message to Chinese: some ethnic minorities have demonstrated demographic advantages over the Han ethnic group in some fields.

Remarkable Research on the Tibetan Population

Tibetan population problems have attracted great attention from many scholars both at home and abroad due to its special, mysterious and sensitive nature. It has become a research focus since the 1980s.

Research has identified the following problems with the Tibetan population:

The first is population size. Agreement on the largest population reached in Tibetan history varies significantly. Some say the number is 945,000, some say 6,000,000, while others say it used to be as large as 10 million or even 33 million. Before the 1950s in Tibet, there was no household registration system or census. However, the first census China did in 1953 recorded the Tibetan population to be 1 million, based on reports by the local Tibetan government led by the Dalai Lama.

Secondly, problems concerning marriage, birth and death are considered to be severe. According to the 1990 census, many of the problems stem from its elderly population (those born before 1930). Of this demographic, the non-marriage rate among women aged from 65 to 69 was reported at 10.8 percent; the prevalence of lifetime infertility among women aged from 60 to 64 was 17.7 percent, 16.3 percentage points higher than the national average; the fertility rate of Tibetan women at the childbearing age prior to the democratic reform in 1959 flulctuated between 3.01 to 3.85, which was a striking contrast against the natural birth rate of more than 5.0 at home and abroad. In 1951, infant mortality in Tibet was as high as 430 per thousand and the average life expectancy was only 35 year old.

Thirdly, complete absence of modern education. Before the 1950s, there was not a single modern school in Tibet because Tibetan monastic education was the mainstream. The adult illiteracy rate was as high as 90.6 percent, with 80 percent among men and 97.6 percent among women.

During the second half of the 20th century, the Tibetan population, however, underwent several changes.

First, Tibetan population growth accelerated significantly. In the second census in 1964, the total population in Tibet was 1.251 million, among which 1.209 million were Tibetans; in the third census in 1982, the total population in Tibet was 1.892 million, among which 1.786 million were Tibetans; in

The Tibetan women in the streets of Lhasa, Tibet.

the fourth census in 1990, the total population in Tibet was 2.196 million, among which 2.096 million were Tibetans.

Since 1970, the birth rate and natural population growth rate have both been higher than the national avereages. From 1982 to 1990, the Tibetan population in Tibet increased by 309,800, with a natural growth rate of 17.34 per thousand, 2.64 per thousand higher than the average natural national growth over the same period.

At the same time, Tibetans have always accounted for an overwhelming majority of the total population in Tibet. In 1982, the Han people and other ethnic minorities accounted for 4.85 percent and 0.75 percent of the total population in Tibet Autonomous Region, respectively; in 1982, the Han people and other ethnic minorities accounted for 3.68 percent and 0.82 percent; and in 1996, both numbers decreased to 2.9 percent and 0 .8 percent, respectively.

Since the 1950s, the health care industry including Tibetan medicine and modern medicine has been developing quickly. Tibet, the only region in mainland China where the entire population enjoys free medical services, has seen decreases in its death rate from 28 percent in 1951 to 11.6 percent in 1967; to 9.72 percent in 1981 and 7.4 percent in 1990. Meanwhile, the infant mortality rate decreased from 430 per thousand in 1951 to 155.2 per thousand in 1981, 136.0 per thousand in 1987 and 97.4 per thousand in 1990; while the death rate of pregnant women decreased from 50 per thousand in 1951 to 14.3 per thousand in 1985, to 5.7 per thousand in 1994. The average life expectancy in Tibet increased from 35 in 1951, to 56.95 in 1987, and to 59.61 in 1990.

From 1982 to 1995, the proportion of college-educated people in Tibetan population increased from 0.42 percent to 0.78 percent, but it was still much lower than the national average of 2.03 percent. The illiteracy rate of people more than 15 years of age dropped to 61.50 percent, but the figure was still 45 percentage points higher than the national average of 16.48 percent. Meanwhile, the overall average education level increased to 2.19, accounting for 34.76 percent of the national average. Therefore, there is still a long way to go with improving the education level in Tibet.

Latest Trends of Population Mobility

On Sept 18, 2002, two Luoba people from Tibet settled in China Folk Culture Village in Shenzhen. This was not a trifle event for Shenzhen—before this event, people from 54 ethnic minorities, totaling 220,000 people, were living in Shenzhen; after this event, however, Shenzhen became the second city, apart from Beijing, to have 55 ethnic minorities living together in one city.

It merely took Shenzhen, the frontier city of reform and opening up in China, 20 years to become such a city. In 1982,

Representatives of 56 ethnic groups from all social circles of Shenzhen are taking pictures together happily.

there were 372 ethnic minority people in Shenzhen; and over 225,000 in 2002, an increase of 600 times. At the same time, Shenzhen's total population grew only by about 35 times.

The progress of reform and opening up is also the process of a massive number of ethnic minority people moving to urban and coastal areas. As such there are many other cities similar to Shenzhen in this aspect.

While Beijing was the first city to have people from 55 ethnic minorities living together, by 2008, there had been people from 53 ethnic minorities living together in Shanghai, and 37 ethnic minorities in Changchun and Shenyang.

Ethnic minority populations are increasing dramatically in coastal areas in China where traditionally there were not many ethnic minorities living. The autonomous region of Guangxi has the largest ethnic minority population in China, and from 1990 to 2000, the ethnic minority population in Guangxi grew by 3.82 percent, while its neighboring province Guangdong—a coastal province that ranks high in China for its economic development—its ethnic minority population increased by 246 percent over the same period. At the same time, the coastal provinces of Zhejiang and Jiangsu, which have a relatively higher level of economic development, also saw its ethinic minority populations grow by over 50 percent.

According to statistics released by China's ethnic affairs departments since the 1980s, there have been around 9 million transient and permanent ethnic minority people living in urban areas in China, forming compact communities of different sizes.

All the facts mentioned above have added a new key phrase in China's work on ethnic minorities after the reform and opening up: Ethnic Work in Urban Areas.

Protecting the rights of ethnic minorities has become the centerpiece of ethnic work in urban areas. Because of spatial distance and cultural as well as psychological differences, how migrant ethnic minority people and local residents adapt to each other is often a complicated process. This makes ethnic minority work in urban areas rather difficult and particularly sensitive in China. In this practice, the country aims to guarantee the rights of migrant ethnic minority people in urban areas by formulating relevant laws and regulations.

Regional Ethnic Autonomy in China

China's Ethnic Policy in Trudeau's Eyes

Pierre Elliott Trudeau (1919–2000) is known as the most famous politician in Canadian history, who has twice served as Prime Minister of Canada. In 1960, when he was a commentator on current affairs living in the province of Quebec, Trudeau and his friend Jacques Hebert (1923–2007) came to visit China at the Chinese government's invitation.

Trudeau and Hebert, who later became a Canadian senator, stayed in China for one month and toured around the country from Changchun in the north to Guangzhou in the south. In Beijing, when asked what they wished to see in China, Trudeau replied: "Canadians are different from other people, and we are very interested in issues concerning China's ethnic minorities."

At the time, Canada was gradually slipping into conflicts among ethnic groups, disputes over languages and constitutional disagreements. Ethnic problems had become the political debate at the heart of the Canadian government.

The two guests were invited to visit the Central Academy of National Minorities. About what they saw in the place responsible for the education of ethnic minority intellectuals they said: "No doubt, this small world is full of happiness in life." Trudeau and Hebert later wrote down everything they observed in China in a book titled *TwoInnocents in Red China*. Its fifth chapter "Ethnic Minorities in China" was devoted to their visit to the Central Academy of National Minorities.

Certainly, Trudeau and Hebert's understanding of China's ethnic policy did not come solely from the Central Academy of National Minorities. The two Canadian friends strived to understand more about China's ethnic issues and policies. In their book they wrote: "From the perspective of the Chinese government structure, ethnic minorities have more seats than they are supposed to have: the total population of 51 ethnic minorities was only 38 million (the ethnic identification in China had not been completed in 1960, so only 51 ethnic minorities had been identified), accounting for 6 percent of the total population of China; however, they have 14.5 percent representative seats in the National People's Congress. The powerful Chinese government does not try to convert ethnic minorities but strives to preserve their ethnic minority features instead, especially their languages."

"Shortly after liberation, of 51 ethnic minorities only 21 had their own written languages. Linguists created 16 kinds of languages and improved three kinds. China's linguistic problems being so complicated, their practice makes me think that we should indeed give a serious consideration to their policy, which does not take the path of cultural assimilation but strives to ensure that these new languages be able to exist for ever," the two Canadians wrote.

The Hui people living in Beijing are voting for representatives of the National People' Congress.

In effect, the ethnic minority policy that China employed in terms of language had astonished and shocked both Trudeau and Hebert. In Canada at the time, the status dispute between English and French alone had already made it difficult to bring the complicated situation under control. In China, however, the government went as far as to create languages for ethnic groups who did not have one.

In the 1960s, China encountered a series of "misunderstandings and refusals to understand" due to the Cold War situation. But Trudeau and Hebert saw several things in this very country which made their stances objective.

"A tiny coincidence has enabled us to note a few conclusive signs. When studying 'The National Agricultural Development Plan', we read such content in the 24th clause that the family planning policy must be publicized in sparsely populated areas, except ethnic for minority regions," they also wrote.

Two authors admitted that in China: "Ethnic minorities do live a better life than those in Western countries where economic factors rule everything."

The last paragraph of the fifth chapter in *Two Innocents in Red China* reads: "People in Quebec will discover in the end that what Ottawa needs to learn from Beijing is more than a lesson."

Why Has China Employed Regional Ethnic Autonomy Rather than Federalism?

People familiar with the history of the Communist Party of China may know that the CPC proposed to establish a federal country in history. It was put forth at the Second National Congress of the Communist Party of China in 1922: "Based on the principle of free federalism, the Federal Republic of China, which includes Mongolia, Tibet and Xinjiang, will be established." It was also put forth in the Seventh National Congress of the Communist Party of China in 1945: "Based on the principle of willingness and democracy, all ethnic groups in China shall establish the Federal Republic of China and organize the central government on the basis of this federal system."

However, when the People's Republic of China was founded, the Chinese government employed ethnic regional autonomy rather than federalism.

The Communist Party of China proposed to adopt federalism in its early days due to the great impact upon China from the Soviet socialist revolution. After the October Revolution, the Soviet government adopted a federal system to maintain the solidarity and unity of its all ethnic groups which used to be under the rule of the former Tsarist Russia. After the founding of the People's Republic of China, the government's decision to adopt regional ethnic autonomy was based on a more realistic understanding and awareness of China's national conditions during the long practice of social revolution.

The Communist Party of China began to understand ethnic problems during the Long March from 1934 to 1936. Of the 25,000 *li* (one *li* equals to half a kilometer) covered by the Red Army, a considerable part of the distance was located in ethnic minority regions. According to statistics, 13 ethnic minorities were scattered around the places that the Red Army passed—the Miao, Yao, Zhuang, Dong, Bouyei, Tujia, Bai, Naxi, Yi, Qiang, Hui, Tibetan and Yugur minorities. Because the Red Army treated ethnic minorities in conformation with the principle of equality, they received genuine help from ethnic minorities during the difficult journey; at the same time, the Red Army also helped the Yi and Tibetan minorities set up several ethnic minority regimes that were autonomous in nature.

A deeper problem of the ethnic minority debate beame rooted during the War of Resistance against Japanese aggression. During its all-around invasion of China, Japan instigated three northwestern provinces of Gansu, Qinghai, and Ningxia to establish of a puppet regime called "*Da Hui Hui Guo*" (Great Hui State), in order to further occupy China's territory. At that time, the Communist Party of China, which had set up a border region regime in the northwestern city of Yan'an, initiated timely research into the Mongol and *Hui* minorities in this region. A group of Party members who began working on ethnic affairs earlier drafted the *Outline of Questions Concerning the Hui Minority* and the *Outline of Questions Concerning the Mongol Minority*, after understanding their history, politics, economy and culture in a broad and thorough context. The two documents were the start of a series of research work into ethnic minority issues by the Communist Party of China. Subsequently, in May of 1941 the Shaanxi-Gansu-Ningxia Border Region Government included the policy of ethnic regional autonomy in its newly-issued Administrative Program in the Shanxi-Gansu-Ningxia Border Region. The program clearly stated: "Under the principle of equality among ethnic groups, the Mongol, Hui and Han ethnic groups have equal political, economic and cultural rights, and the Mongolian and Hui autonomous regions will be founded."

This was the first attempt by the Communist Party of China to solve domestic ethnic issues through the policy of ethnic regional autonomy.

The border region government also put its Administrative Program into real practice. A number of regional and township regimes called the "Hui Autonomous Region" and the "Mongolian Autonomous Region" were set up one after another. These regimes enjoyed the following rights: they could organize a government mainly consisting of their own ethnic representatives by voting; they could establish ethnic minority anti-Japanese military forces with independent rights of military actions; there must be ethnic minority representatives in the border region, county and township councils; economically, the border region government shall provide financial handouts to assist autonomous regions in production, with all burdens eliminated; in terms of culture and education, they could establish cultural agencies for autonomous ethnic groups, public primary schools for the Hui ethnic group and provide free education.

The primary policy of ethnic autonomy included a great number of decrees concerning religious freedom, respect for ethnic folklores and use of ethnic spoken and written languages. In order to meet religious requirements of the Hui people, the border region government carefully chose a site and constructed a mosque. The stone tablet in front of the mosque bore the inscription of the mosque's name written by Chairman Mao; and the inauguration ceremony was conducted in accordance with Muslim rituals and practices. That day, the Imam in Yan'an hosted a solemn ritual and all Muslims knelt and bowed in the mosque. Important leaders of the Communist Party of China such as Zhu De (1886–1976), Xie Juezai (1884–1971), Li Weihan (1896–1984) attended the ceremony.

Representatives of ethnic minorities at the National People's Congress.

In the 1940s it became a prevalent practice in Yan'an to respect ethnic history and tradition. There was a unique building Genghis Khan Memorial by the Yanshui River. Evidently, this was constructed for Mongolians exclusively. Public memorial ceremonies dedicated to Genghis Khan (1162–1227), the Mongolian ancestor, were held here both in the winter and summer every year.

During this period, the most important result of the implementation of ethnic regional autonomy by the Communist Party of China was the establishment of the first provincial ethnic autonomous region in 1947: Inner Mongolia Autonomous Region.

Despite a great many practices of ethnic regional autonomy, at the critical point when the PRC was to be founded, leaders of the Communist Party of China still raised this question solemnly: will the New China adopt federalism, or ethnic regional autonomy under the rule of a united republic? After thorough research, the final conclusion was: China had a different national condition from Russia, and thus should not adopt federalism.

The biggest difference between China and Russia was that the ethnic minority population in Russia, accounting for 47 percent of Russia's total population, almost equated the population of the Russian majority; while in China, the total population of ethnic minorities only accounted for 6 percent of China's total population. Furthermore, the Han and ethnic minorities had long been living in mixture or in adjacent compact communities in history, which was completely different from Russia. Second, after the February and October Revolutions, in fact, many non-Russian minorities split into different countries, most of which became Soviet countries after civil wars, so Bolshevik had to adopt federalism as a transitory model to unite all Soviet countries for outright unification. In China, all ethnic groups teamed up equally and participated in democratic revolutions against imperialism and dictatorship until the People's Republic was founded on the basis of equality, while before China had been a unified country all the time without any phase of ethnic separation.

Therefore: "The People's Republic of China shall adopt ethnic regional autonomy rather than federalism," was submitted as a founding program to the First Chinese People's Political Consultative Conference held in September 1949 to be discussed by all members of the CPPCC.

The First Chinese People's Political Consultative Conference, which was held before the founding of the People's Republic of China, included discussions of extraordinary significance. At the meeting a series of crucial principle matters that the country should follow were discussed and a consensus

● Data Link

Milestones in China's Ethnic Regional Autonomy

In February of 1952, the first decree on ethnic regional autonomy—the Outline for the Implementation of Ethnic Regional Autonomy in the PRC was released. It symbolized that China's ethnic regional autonomy had embarked on the jurisdiction of law.

In September of 1954, ethnic regional autonomy was written into the first Constitution of PRC, and Ethnic Regional Autonomy was named one of the basic political systems in China.

In May of 1984, the Law of the People's Republic of China on Ethnic Regional Autonomy was officially issued and carried out as of October 1 of the same year.

In September 1997, on the Fifteenth National Congress of the Communist Party of China, ethnic regional autonomy together with the system of National People's Congress and the system of multi-party cooperation and political consultation led by the Communist Party of China formed the three basic political systems in China. This further acknowledged the important role that ethnic regional autonomy played in the national political system.

In February of 2001, the Twelfth Session of the Ninth National People's Congress passed the amendments to the Law of the People's Republic of China on Ethnic Regional Autonomy.

was reached by representatives elected by all parties, associations and ethnic groups. Concerning what structure the future country should adopt, representatives at the conference held serious and careful talks and finally decided to establish the People's Republic under a unitary system in China.

"Compact communities of ethnic minorities shall implement ethnic regional autonomy and set up (different) kinds of ethnic autonomous agencies respectively based on their populations and geographical sizes," wrote the Common Program of the CPPCC, which was passed unanimously at the First Chinese People's Political Consultative Conference and served as the provisional constitution.

In 1954, ethnic regional autonomy was officially written into the first Constitution of the PRC as a basic political system.

Why Do Chinese Pursue National Unity?

Many years later, some researchers noticed that the regional autonomy of ethnic minorities in a unified country was not a random political choice in a particular time for a particular region. They pointed to the fact that it was inherently determined by Chinese historical and cultural traditions over several millenniums.

In fact, national unity, which is deeply rooted in Chinese historical tradition over several thousands of years, has been the everlasting common inspiration of all Chinese people. Since the Qin and Han dynasties, despite confrontations and disputes among different ethnic groups, national unity has been the mainstream of historical development even with periods of separation and disunion. Integrated in a united nation, different ethnic groups developed close relationships of interdependence through political, economic and cultural communications. Moreover, a strong sense of national solidarity and common pursuit of national unity

Urumqi, capital
of Xinjiang Uygur
Autonomous
Region.

flourished. In modern times, in the fight against imperialism, all the ethnic groups experienced the twists and turns together, thus fostering an inseparable relationship on the basis of existing cooperation. Furthermore, safeguarding the unity of the nation has ever since become an irreversible historical trend.

Ancient Chinese history shows us that national prosperity comes along with national unity. During its crest historical stages such as the Han, Tang, and Qing dynasties, national strength was always coupled with national unity. With such a national historic backdrop, national unity has become the ultimate pursuit of all ethnic groups.

An intriguing phenomenon is that in spite of huge cultural gaps among different ethnic groups, China stands as a single sovereignty in modern world history. The coexistence of diversity and consistency of Chinese culture is not imposed by human factors; instead, it is therefore both a result of the choices made in Chinese history and decisions made during the long accumulation of Chinese culture.

Ethnic Groups and Religions in China

Ethnic Autonomous Areas in China

In early 1952, Chairman Mao sent a message to Seypidin Azizi (1915–2003) who was far away in Xinjiang. It said: "Please offer your detailed proposal on the issue of regional autonomy of Xinjiang."

In his report, he replied Chairman Mao with his own ideas on the main tasks and constituents of the Xinjiang autonomous government. In particular, he suggested that the name of the future government be called Xinjiang Uygur Autonomous Government.

On October 1, 1955, Xinjiang Uygur Autonomous Region was established. Azizi was elected the Chairman of the People's Committee and Secretary of Party Committee of Xinjiang Uygur Autonomous Region.

Xinjiang is the first provincial autonomous region after the establishment of People Republic of China. In the next decade, three more would follow: on March 5, 1958, Guangxi Zhuang Autonomous Region, on October 25, 1958, Ningxia

Yinchuan, capital of Ningxia Hui Autonomous Region.

Hui Autonomous Region, and on September 9, 1965, Tibet Autonomous Region.

Together with Inner Mongolia Autonomous Region founded in 1947, before the founding of the PRC, there were five provincial autonomous regions in China. The organizational system of those autonomous regions was arranged in the hierarchy of an autonomous region, autonomous prefecture and autonomous county.

The first autonomous prefecture founded by the People's Republic of China was the Tibetan Autonomous Prefecture of Garze, which Sichuan established in November of 1950. The Enshi Tujia and Miao Autonomous Prefecture in Hubei was established in December 1983, and is the youngest prefecture in the country.

Currently, the country has 30 autonomous prefectures.

In May of 1950, the first autonomous county—the Tianzhu Tibetan Autonomous County in Gansu Province was founded. Meanwhile, the Beichuan Qiang Autonomous County in Mianyang, Sichuan declared its establishment in July of 2003, becoming the youngest autonomous county in China.

To date there are 120 autonomous counties in China.

From a general point of view, the autonomous areas fall into the following categories:

(1) Autonomous areas are established in places where one ethnic minority lives in a compact community, such as in Xinjiang Uygur Autonomous Region.

(2) Autonomous areas are established in places where two ethnic minorities live in compact communities, such as

in Hunan's Xiangxi Tujia and Miao Autonomous Prefecture.

(3) Autonomous areas are established in places where several ethnic minorities live in compact communities, such as the Jishishan Bao'an, Dongxian and Salar Autonomous County in Linxia Hui Autonomous Prefecture, Gansu Province.

(4) Autonomous areas are established within a larger autonomous area where people from an ethnic minority with a smaller population live in compact communities, such as the Ili Kazak Autonomous Prefecture in Xinjiang Uygur Autonomous Region; and the Qabqal Xibo Autonomous County in Ili Kazak Autonomous Prefecture.

(5) Autonomous areas established for one ethnic minority which lives in compact communities in different places, such as the Hui minority in Ningxia Hui Autonomous Region, Linxia Hui Autonomous Prefecture in Gansu Province and Dachang Hui Autonomous County in Hebei Province. Another example is the Miao minority, which establishes or co-establishes 13 autonomous counties and six prefectures around the country.

In China today, 44 of 55 ethnic minorities have established autonomous areas. Autonomous area populations account for 71 percent of the entire population of all ethnic minorities.

The ethnic township is another administrative organization that comprises Chinese characteristics. As a supplement to autonomous areas, ethnic townships are established in places where ethnic minorities live in compact communities, where autonomous governments are not fit to be established because the areas and populations of the ethnic minorities are too small.

According to the Regulations on the Administrative Work of Ethnic Townships, heads of the ethnic townships should be citizens from the ethnic minorities exercising regional autonomy in the area concerned, and other members of the people's governments of these townships shall include a proportion of members of the ethnic group exercising regional autonomy.

The country has nine ethnic townships in places where autonomous governments cannot be established because the areas and populations of the ethnic minorities are too small. There are currently 1,100 ethnic townships in the country.

▶ Data Link

Brief Introduction of the Five Autonomous Regions in China

Inner Mongolia Autonomous Region

In all, 49 ethnic groups live on a land of 1.183 million sq km; it boasts a total population of 23.9235 million (as of 2006), among which 4.2338 million are Mongolians. Three autonomous counties in this region are: Oroqen Autonomous County, Ewenke Autonomous County and Morin Dawa Daur Autonomous County.

Xinjiang Uygur Autonomous Region

It covers an area of 16,649 sq km inhabited by 47 ethnic groups, among which 13 are natives. By 2006, it had a population of 20.5 million with 60.4 percent comprising ethnic minorities. It includes five autonomous prefectures, six autonomous counties and 43 ethnic townships.

Guangxi Zhuang Autonomous Region

It covers an area of 236,700 sq km populated by the greatest number of ethnic groups including a dozen native ethnic groups. As the home of the largest proportion of the *Yao* and Mulam minorities, it is also the only region where the Jing minority lives.

Ningxia Hui Autonomous Region

It covers an area of 51,800 sq km inhabited by 35 ethnic groups. Among a population of 6.12 million people, 1.8625 million are from the the Hui minority, accounting for 18.9 percent of all Hui people in China (as of 2007). Two-thirds of the population in Ningxia is made up of the Han ethnic group who have been native inhabitants since ancient times.

Tibet Autonomous Region

It covers an area of 1.20223 million sq km with a population of 2.81 million and a density of 2.21 people/sq km (as of 2006). Most of the population lives in the southern and eastern part of the region. With the Tibetan minority as the largest one, Tibet is also the only region where the Monba and Lhoba minorities settle.

Main Ideas of the Law of the People's Republic of China on Ethnic Regional Autonomy

The law includes seven chapters or 74 articles. Its core point is pertains to the autonomous rights of the autonomous areas, which is summarized as follows:

I. Organs of autonomous governments in autonomous areas

Organs of autonomous governments in autonomous areas are the people's congresses and people's governments of autonomous regions, autonomous prefectures and autonomous counties.

Dec 11, 2008, the 50th anniversary of the establishment of Guangxi Zhuang Autonomous Region.

The organs of autonomous governments in autonomous areas shall apply the System of People's Congress.

The people's governments of autonomous areas shall apply the system that gives overall responsibility to the chairman of autonomous regions, the prefect of an autonomous prefecture and the head of an autonomous county, who shall direct the work of the people's governments at their respective levels.

The chairman of an autonomous region, the governor of an autonomous prefecture and the head of an autonomous county shall be a citizen of the ethnic group exercising regional autonomy in the area concerned.

Among the chairman or vice-chairmen of the standing committee of the people's congress of an autonomous area there shall be one or more citizens from the ethnic group or groups exercising regional autonomy in the area concerned.

In the people's congress of an autonomous region, autonomous prefecture or autonomous county, in addition to the representatives of the ethnic group exercising regional autonomy in the administrative area, other ethnic groups inhabiting the area are also entitled to appropriate representation. Ethnic minorities with small populations will enjoy favorable policies in terms of the number and proportion of representatives.

The cadres in regional autonomous goverments as well as their subsidiary departments shall, whenever possible, include citizens from the ethnic minority group exercising regional autonomy in the area. Priority should be given to ethnic minority cadres who meet the basic requirements.

In autonomous areas where the populations of ethnic minorities reach or exceed half of the entire local population, the number of cadres shall be kept to an appropriate proportion; in autonomous areas where populations of ethnic minorities is less than half of the entire local population, there should be a higher proportion of cadres from ethnic minorities.

II. Power of autonomous governments in ethnic autonomous areas

(1) Legislative power

People's congresses in autonomous areas have the right to formulate autonomous regulations and other separate regulations in light of the special political, economic and cultural conditions of the ethnic group in that autonomous area.

Autonomous regulations stipulate basic issues on regional autonomy; while separate regulations should deal mainly with issues on regional autonomy in a specific field.

Autonomous regulations and separate regulations may contain provisions which have been properly altered on the basis of existing laws or administrative regulations.

(2) Flexible enforcement

If a resolution, decision, order or instruction of a state organ at a higher level does not suit the conditions in a national autonomous area, the organ of an autonomous government in the area may either implement certain modifications or cease implementation after having reported to and received the approval of the state organs at a higher level.

(3) Independent economic development

Autonomous organs in autonomous areas shall enjoy more independence in finance and economy as well as State preferential treatment; they can also open ports for foreign trade after obtaining approval from the State Council

(4) Autonomy in administering finance

All revenues accruing to the ethnic autonomous area shall be managed and used by the organs of autonomous governments. If the expenditures of an ethnic autonomous area exceed its revenues, subsidies shall be granted by the financial department at a higher level. All ethnic autonomous areas enjoy different kinds of special subsidies and provisional allowances granted by the State. While implementing tax laws of the State, the organs of autonomous governments in ethnic autonomous areas may grant tax exemptions or reductions for certain items which should be encouraged or given preferential consideration in taxation, except for items on which tax reduction or exemption require unified examination and approval by the State.

(5) Autonomy in culture, spoken and written languages

Organs of autonomous governments in ethnic autonomous areas shall enjoy certain cultural autonomy. It ensures the freedom of using and developing the spoken and written languages of every ethnic group in the concerned areas.

While performing its functions, the organ of the autonomous government in an ethnic autonomous area shall, in accordance with the regulations on the exercise of autonomy of the area, use one or several commonly used languages in the locality; when several common languages are used for the performance of such functions, the language of the ethnic group exercising regional autonomy may be used as the main language.

(6) Organizing local public security forces

Organs of autonomous governments in autonomous areas may, in accordance with the military system of the State and practical local needs, organize local public security forces to maintain public order after being approved by the State Council,

(7) Independent development of science and technology, education and culture

Organs of autonomous governments in ethnic autonomous areas have the right to make plans for educational development in these areas, to open various kinds of schools and determine their educational plans, systems, forms, curricula, teaching languages, and enrollment procedures. Organs of autonomous governments in ethnic autonomous areas shall independently develop literature, art, newscasting, publishing, radio broadcasting, the film industry, television and other ethnic cultural undertakings both in forms and with characteristics unique to these ethnic minorities; they shall further decide on plans for the development of science and technology in these areas, shall make independent decisions on plans for developing local medical and healthcare services, shall make their own decisions when it comes to the development of traditional ethnic sports activities, and shall protect local scenic spots, historical sites and precious cultural relics.

The Power of Autonomous Government Organs: the Tibet Case

In accordance with the Law of the People's Republic of China on Ethnic Regional Autonomy, Tibet enjoys regional autonomy including legislative power. Meanwhile, Tibet Autunomous Region may make flexible modifications when implementing existing laws or administrative regulations in light of local conditions

Since its establishment, Tibet Autunomous Region has formulated over 150 regulations, resolutions, decisions and orders on the basis of historic, cultural and natural features of Tibetan heritage.

Examples of this are the autonomous area's designated holidays, which include the Tibetan New Year, the Shoton (Yogurt) Festival and other traditional Tibetan festivals that are marked as official regional holidays, separate from the country's official national holidays. In addition, in consideration of the special natural and geographical factors of Tibet, Tibet Autonomous Region has fixed the work week at 35 hours, five hours fewer than the national statutory work week.

These stipulations and rules make clear that:

The flag-raising ceremony in Potala Palace Square in Lhasa, Tibet.

(1) Tibetan Language is the commonly used language in Tibet; equal attention shall be given to Tibetan language and Chinese in Tibet Autonomous Region, with the Tibetan language as the major one.

(2) All the resolutions and regulations by the people's congresses at various levels in Tibet, and formal documents and public announcements of the governments at all levels in Tibet Autonomous Region are printed in both Tibetan and Chinese languages.

(3) Newspapers, radios and TV programs in Tibet are all in both the Tibetan language and Chinese.

(4) All signs and logos for government agencies, roads, traffic sign posts and public facilities should be written in both Tibetan language and Chinese.

(5) In judicial lawsuits when Tibetans are involved, the Tibetan language is used both in the trial and in the writing of legal documents.

In 1981, considering the tradition of polyandrous and

polygamous marriages of the Tibetan minority, Tibet Autonomous Region adopted the "Accommodation Rules for the Implementation of the Marriage Law of the People's Republic of China," which stipulates that polyandrous and polygamous marriages formed before the promulgation of the "Accommodation Rules" shall be valid if none of the persons involved takes initiative to terminate the marriage. In accordance with the "Accommodation Rules," those who carry on the tradition of polyandrous and polygamous marriages, monogamy persuasions shall be given while bigamy will not be involved.

The "Accommodation Rules" also lower the statutory marriage age by two years as provided by the Marriage Law according to historic tradition. In Tibet, only males over 20 and females over 18 can legally wed.

Amendments to the Law of the People's Republic of China on Ethnic Regional Autonomy

China's market economy was initiated in the 1980s, and matured quickly in the 90s. With such rapid economic development, it became inevitable amendments would be needed to the former Law of the People's Republic of China on Ethnic Regional Autonomy, which had been created under the planned economy.

Calls for its revision revolve around the economic regulations stipulated under the planned economy. Meanwhile, in the tide of reform and opening up, driven by the unprecedented aspiration for economic progress in ethnic autonomous areas, ethnic minorities urgently demand the law represent their wishes for economic growth.

The 90s witnessed the start of the amendment process, and after nearly a decade of research and investigation, the revised Law of the People's Republic of China on Ethnic

Regional Autonomy was finally published in 2001.

A major change lies in the emphasis on the central government's responsibility to help ethnic minorities with local economic growth. The revised version clearly stipulates that developed areas should offer paired-up assistance to ethnic autonomous areas. Among the 31 amended articles, 23 revolve around the topics of social and economic development.

For example, the newly added Article 56 stipulates: The State shall, in accordance with unified planning and market demand, give top priority to ethnic autonomous areas when making rational arrangements for resource development projects and infrastructure projects. Meanwhile, Article 57 states: The State shall, in the light of the characteristics and needs of economic development in ethnic autonomous areas, make comprehensive use of the monetary market and the capital market to increase its monetary support to the areas. Finally, Article 69 states: The state and the people's

Nadam Festival of Inner-Mongolia. Nadam is a traditional Mongolian festival.

governments at higher levels shall provide greater support for the poverty-stricken areas in ethnic autonomous areas in the financial, monetary, material, technological and trained personnel fields so as to help the poor populations in the concerned areas shake off poverty as soon as possible to allow them to reach their full potential.

The amendments also add that the State shall give economic compensations to ethnic autonomous areas that produce natural resources.

Unique "Chinese Model"

The international community employs the term "Chinese model" to describe China's practice of using ethnic regional autonomy to solve ethnic issues.

Since the second half of the 20th century, against the backdrop of worldwide ethnic confrontations, China's regional ethnic autonomy has shown its special value. As a unique "China Model," it has attracted increasing attention from the international community.

Many foreign scholars and politicians have stated that: China's ethnic regional autonomy not only shows the consensus of protecting the interests of minorities but also puts this into practice. China's experiences show a wise solution to ethnic issues for countries around the world, and cast new light on political activities in solving ethnic issues, providing an enormous contribution to the arena of international politics.

China's Ethnic Minority Culture as Well as Its Protection and Development

Cultural Self-identity, Cultural Tolerance, Cultural Coexistence and Common Prosperity

In December 1990, the International Conference of East Asian Studies was held in Tokyo by Japanese sociologists to celebrate the 80th birthday of Fei Xiaotong. In his keynote speech, "Research on Humans in China—Personal Experiences," he proposed concepts known as "cultural self-identity, cultural tolerance, cultural coexistence and common prosperity."

It is not easy to translate his words to anther language because of its phonologic and grammatical beauty, which can only be appreciated by Chinese speakers. However, the world should know its connotation.

"Cultural self identity" indicates cultural self-acknowledgement: each culture has its own values, and should be

Twelve Muqam of Xinjiang Uygurs.

Tibetan Opera Performance.

acknowledged respectfully by another culture.

"Cultural tolerance" means the attitude towards a foreign culture: in front of an exotic culture, each culture should be tolerant of cultural differences, and admit and appreciate the beauty of other cultures.

"Cultural coexistence and common prosperity" suggests the connection between various cultures, that is, to respect and coexist with each other in harmony despite having different values. Differences in harmony will bring vitality, and that diversity coexists with order, and unity is the ideal state of the world.

"Cultural coexistence" originates from traditional Chinese philosophy of "Harmony in

Chinese Korean farmers' music and dance.

Diversity." The great thought is also a conclusion of long-term studies on ethnic relations by Fei Xiaotong. It is the golden rule of cultural coexistence; likewise, it is also the best principle for the harmonious interaction of civilizations.

"56 Ethnic Groups Are like 56 Flowers Flourishing in the Garden of China"

The late Canadian Prime Minister Pierre Elliott Trudeau believed that the Chinese government holds a "cautious respect" in ethnic issues. Behind this attitude lies the principle that "ethnic groups, big or small, are all equal," which is exactly the basic attitude of Chinese government towards the culture of ethnic minorities.

As sung in a well-known song—*56 ethnic groups, 56 flowers*, all 56 ethnic groups are likened to 56 flowers. If we compare flowers to ethnic culture, the song has a deeper meaning. In China, people tend to call the coexistence of diversity "let hundred flowers blossom."

Liang Tingwang, who put forward the theory of "cultural plates" holds that: Chinese culture contains four parts: agricultural civilization in the Central Plain; nomadic culture in northern grasslands; agricultural and nomadic culture in southwest China; and rice culture in southern China. Based on the above four plates is a rich variety of 56 ethnic cultures.

But the mere general descriptions of cultural diversity of ethnic minorities are not enough. We will get a deeper

Water-Splashing Festival of the Dai People.

impression from the following detailed analysis about its variety and diversity.

Examples of Cultural Diversity of Ethnic Minorities in China

Epics of ethnic minorities

German philosopher Georg Wilhelm Friedrich Hegel (1770–1831) once asserted in *Aesthetics* that China had no epics.

But he was wrong.

China not only has epics but also owns the longest epics in the world.

The Tibetan epic *Gesar* is still alive—it is even growing in the performance, dialogue and singing of folk artists.

Dating back 1,000 years ago, *Gesar* is the collective wisdom of all Tibetans. It includes over 120 volumes, that is, 1 million lines or 20 million words, longer than all five famous epics in the world combined. (The five epics are the ancient Babylonian *Gelgamesh*, *Iliad* and *Odyssey* of Ancient Greece, and *Ramayana* and *Mahabarata* of Hindustan). *Gesar* depicts the general picture of society and history, religious beliefs, communications between different ethnic groups, social morality and folk customs; it is considered the encyclopedia of the ancient Tibetan minority.

For thousands of years, *Gesar* has been passed on by peasants and herdsmen living in remote areas. How could they recite thousands of lines? How do they learn to sing? How do they memorize these words? These questions still linger around known as the "Sphinx Myth" in *Gesar* studies.

Among the chanters, old Zhaba is a legend. He created 25 volumes of *Gesar*, which contain 600,000 lines or 6 million words. What does such a large number indicate?—It is 25 times as long as Homer's epics.

Epic of Manas of the Kirgiz minority is another living epic which tells the story of how great leaders in eight generations of the Manas family led the people of Kirgiz to fight against foreign oppression. The folk epic, which originated around 9th and 10th century, is over 210,000 lines long, with tens of thousands of people who participated in its composition.

Because of its high reputation in international literature history, the United Nations once designated the year 1995 as "International Manas Year."

Gesar, Manas, and the Mongol minority's *Djangar* constitute the three heroic epics in China. Named after the legendary hero Djangar, it is 60 volumes, or more than 100,000 lines long.

After the founding of the People's Republic of China, researchers on ethnic minority literature collected and discovered about 100 heroic and immigrant epics among 30 southern ethnic minorities, including the Yi, Miao, Zhuang and Dai minorities.

Tibetan folk artist is singing the lyrics of Tibetan epic *Gesar* by acoustic instruments.

The epics vividly conjure up a picture of the creation of the cosmos, the origins of human life, floods and fated calamities, tribal campaigns as well as constant migrations of ancient people. The images and modalities of narration employed by the epics find their marks in later literature, making them an essential part of the culture of ethnic minorities.

Music of ethnic minorities

One thing all 55 ethnic minorities have in common is the love of music. Almost every ethnic minority appreciates music and each has its own music system with unique features.

The Dong minority concentrating in Guizhou boasts a special attitude toward music: for them, songs are knowledge – the more songs one knows, the more knowledgeable he is. Master singers are the most respected people in the Dong minority. In traditional Dong society, people communicate with songs: they sing at work, they sing while resting, they sing to court, and they even establish cooperation among villages through songfests.

Their idea about music sets a typical example of the musical philosophy that all ethnic minorities share. In addition, it is also a marvel in ethnic musical community. The Dong Grand Song is a polyphonic chorus sang by three or more people. As a type of folk music, experts think the structure of Dong Grand Song cannot be more complicated. Without conductors and accompaniments, it is quite amazing for ordinary Dong people to give stunning performances of such a complicated polyphonic chorus.

For a long time, the world music community holds a stereotype that polyphony only exists in the West and China

Dong Grand Song.

has no multi-voice harmony. The choruses composed by the Dong minority and performed in France in 1986 stirred the international music community, who claimed it an extraordinary discovery in Chinese music history.

The Dong Grand Song represent the ethnic music in southern China, and typical northern ethnic musical works are: 12 Uygur Mukam and Mongolian Long-tuned Songs.

We can seldom find music that can be compared with 12 Uygur Mukam. Composed of 360 pieces of vocal and instrumental music, and combining the works of 44 classic poets and numerous folk songs, 12 Uygur Mukam includes 4,492 lines and it takes 24 hours to sing it.

Mukam is folk music which has also spread in Uzbekistan and Tajikistan. However, Uygur Mukam dwarfs them all with its large scale, complete structure, diverse forms and distinctive features. In 2004, UNESCO enlisted Uygur Mukam among the Masterpieces of Oral and Intangible Cultural Heritage of Humanity.

The beauty of Mongolian Long-tuned Songs is beyond description. Accompanied by Morin Huur, the rhythm lingers, so solemn, stirring and heart touching. It is the extension of time and space by human voices.

The themes of the songs are: the vastness of the grasslands, the eternity of nature, the lapse of time, and the brevity of human life and uncertainty of destiny. Like the pastor on the grasslands, the singers bring our soul back to Mother Nature.

The most distinctive singing technique is a tremolo called *nugola* which ranges from those as soft as silk to those as vibrant as horses galloping. All the subtle changes can not be presented in the scores.

In 2004, UNESCO enlisted Mongolian Long-tuned Songs among the Masterpieces of Oral and Intangible Cultural Heritage of Humanity.

Minority medicine

There are many stories proving the glorious history of traditional ethnic medicine. The following legend is a case in point:

In order to test the nine court physicians for whom he spent a lot of money to employ, Trisong Deutsen (742–797) pretended to be ill and stayed in the palace. Then he released a strange edict saying, "Since you are all famous physicians, feeling the pulse is an easy job for you. But I would like you to read my pulse by feeling the thread tied to my wrist."

A Tibetan doctor is feeling a patient's pulse, observing his tongue and diagnosing illnesses.

Then the King ordered someone to tie threads to cat paws and hand them over to court physicians who were confused at reading the pulse through the thread. They wondered whether the King was fatally ill or if there was something wrong with their medical skills. The pulse felt very weak and slow on soft touch, but as strong as ice on close touch, which was like the pulse pattern of cats. Afterwards, the King ordered someone to tie threads to chicken claws and hand them over to the court physicians. After a while, they came to a conclusion that the pulse vibrated on soft touch, and felt very hard on close touch, which was like the pulse pattern of chickens. On the third time, the King asked assistants to tie the thread to a stone mill, and this time the pulse was very deep and they decided it was like stones.

After Sontzen Gampo (617?–650) unified Tibet, sphygmology of traditional Han medicine was introduced into Tibet. Tibetan physicians developed their own pulse taking methods by learning from traditional Chinese medicine and Indian Ayurvedic medicine. The story indicates the mysterious origin of Tibetan pulse taking methods.

The *Four Medical Tantras* is the best proof of the extensiveness and profoundness of Tibetan medicine. The medical classic includes 156 chapters or 240,000 words. It pushes Tibetan medicine to its peak. It doesn't matter if they are experienced Tibetan doctors or students of Tibetan Traditional Medical College, they all start with *The Four Medical Tantras*.

Tibetan medicine is a typical example of ethnic medicine. Surveys over the past 30 years show that among the 55 ethnic minorities, about 20 have their own independent medicine systems. Also, almost each ethnic group has its own healthcare experiences.

Some ethnic groups set up independent medical theoretical systems, leaving many complete classics of traditional medicine, such as the medicine of Tibetan, Mongolian, Uygur, Korean, Dai, Yi and Hui minorities. Although some

The Dai Medicine Hospital in Xishuangbanna, Yunnan.

ethnic minorities don't have their own written languages, they still have mature and original medical experiences and theories. In recent years, under the support of the government, these ethnic minorities sorted out a set of medical theories passed down orally and have systemized them. Ethnic groups such as the Zhuang, Yao, Dong, Tujia minorities, compiled and published their own medical works.

In June 2009, of the 30 Masters of Traditional Chinese Medicine, the first nationwide assessment of such kind, two are from ethnic medical systems, i.e., Chadrel Rinpoche from Tibetan Hospital in Tibet Autonomous Region and Ce Surongzhabu from Inner Mongolia Medical College.

So far, there are nearly 200 ethnic hospitals financed by the central and local governments, and more ethnic specialist clinics have been opened in many areas. Fourteen educational organizations offer ethnic medical courses to train professionals in ethnic medicine. Ethnic medicine examinations of the Tibetan, Mongolian, Uygur, Dai, Korean and Zhuang minorities have been included in the National Qualification Examination for Doctors. The number of ethnic medical experts has reached over 10,000.

Festivals of ethnic minorities

Festivals of Ethnic Minorities in China, published in 1993, reveals a stunning number —from ancient time till now, 56 ethnic groups have more than 1,700 festivals; among them, about 500 are traditional festivals of the Han ethnic group, the remaining 1,200 belong to ethnic minorities.

China has a variety of festivals, and those of ethnic minorities are especially colorful. They fall into the following groups:

Festivals that are relevant to the calendar, season, and phenology. These include Broad season of the Lisu minority,

The Miao girls attending Sister Festival in the mountainous areas of Guizhou.

Kaquewa Festival of Derung minority, Duan Festival of the Sui minority, Noroz Festival of the Kazak minority, and Anie festival of the Daur minority.

Festivals about agricultural activities, like Heaven's Gift Day of the Manchu (Man) minority, Bai's Rice-transplanting Festival, and Hani ethnic minority's New Rice Festival.

Festivals related to rites and sacrifices, such as tribute to Supo by Mongolian, tribute to gods by the Tujia minority, tribute to Obo by the Yugur minority, ceremonies to worship ancestors by the Yi minority, God of Mountain Festival by the Qiang minority, and ceremonies to welcome ancestors by the She minority.

Festivals that are related to religious beliefs, including the Tibetan Shai Fo Festival, Open-door Day and Close-door Day of the Dai minority, Festival of Walking around "Three Holy Temples" of the Bai minority, Gu Zang Festival of the Miao minority, Pan Wang Festival of the Yao minority, Sama Festival of the Dong minority, Hajie Festival of the Jing minority, and Yi Fan Festival of the Mulam minority.

The annual festival for the elderly of the Korean minority.

Festivals in memory of heroes and historical events, such as Lin Wang Festival of the Dong minority, Danu festival of the Yao minority, and Alu Woluo Festival of the Achang minority.

In addition, there are many festivals for socialization and recreation, like the Folk Song Fair of the Zhuang minority, Mongolian Nadam Fair, Moqing Festival of the Daur minority, and March Street of the Bai minority

Without festivals, there is no cultural integration, communication and succession between ethnic minorities. A survey shows that in Guizhou about 40 percent of the population is made up of ethnic minorities; there are more than 365 ethnic festivals. That is to say, in Guizhou, if you like, everyday is festival.

Practices to Protect and Promote Ethnic Minority Cultures in China

The destiny of a nation depends on the destiny of its culture, as culture is the soul that constitutes the substantial existence of a nation.

Therefore, how a government determines the destiny of an ethnic minority largely depends on what policy it adopts to the ethnic minority culture.

China has many unique practices in protecting and promoting the cultures of ethnic minority.

Spoken and written languages

"The government shall help create or improve written languages for ethnic minorities with no written languages of their own, or with incomplete written languages." It was a resolution proposed in 1951, and in the February of the same year, the Government Administration Council made six resolutions after hearing the report of the Visiting Delegation of Central Ensemble of Ethnic Groups. "Help ethnic minorities create and reform their written languages" was the fifth resolution.

In fact, extensive research has already been conducted on languages of ethnic minorities in China. Luo Changpei (1899–1958), a Manchu linguist, organized surveys on ethnic minority languages around China shortly after he was assigned to set up the Institute of Linguistics at the Chinese Academy of Sciences in 1950.

In June 1951, a brand new discipline in China's higher education history, namely ethnic minority languages and literature, was born in the Central Academy of Nationalities (now called Minzu University of China). At almost the same time, the Advisory Committee of National Language Research was founded in Beijing, many of whose members are ethnic minority language linguists. One of the important jobs this committee did was to draft the "Report on Helping Create Written Languages for Ethnic Minorities without Written Languages." The report proposed for ethnic minorities that have their own spoken languages but no written languages or no commonly used written languages, the committee should, according to their will, help them create an alphabetic written language or choose one from the present applicable written languages after extensive research.

In 1956 another larger census on ethnic minority languages was carried out under the direct leadership of the State Ethnic Affairs Commission. Seven teams of over 700 linguists went to ethnic minority regions. This was the largest census on ethnic minority languages.

The census lasted for over two years. As a result, nearly 40 languages were presented in their phonological systems, vocabularies and grammatical structures, providing scientific foundation for the upcoming creation of written languages.

The Institute of Linguistics, Chinese Academy of Sciences and State Ethnic Affairs Commission decided to choose one ethnic group for the test-run creation of written languages. That group was the Zhuang minority. In December 1957, Premier Zhou Enlai (1898–1976) presided over the 63rd Plenary Meeting of the State Council and the theme was to discuss and approve the proposal on the Zhuang written language.

At the same time, the core program for the creation and reform of written languages—Principals of Designing Letters for Ethnic minority Written Languages—was finally unveiled. It went through several discussions and argumentations before the program was officially formulated.

The design was carried out under very cautious principles, as it not only concerned political equality, but was also a scientific issue—did the newly-created language adhere to the rules of ethnic minority languages? Did it respect the will, feelings and habits of the users? And lastly, the design would affect whether the newly-created language would be accepted and used by ethnic minorities.

After the Zhuang written language was created, 14 language programs for another nine ethnic groups were launched one after another, including for the Buyi, Miao, Yi, Li, Naxi, Lisu, Hani, Wa and Dong ethnic minorities. New programs for the Tu minority in Qinghai, the Tao minority in Guangdong and the Bai minority in Yunnan were formulated in late 1970s and early 1980s.

To improve and reform the existing written languages for some ethnic minorities was another important task. In the 1950s, the government helped the Lahu and Jingpo minorities design reform programs for their written languages and helped the Dai minority design four programs to improve the Dai language.

The creation and reform programs of written languages engaged over 20 million people from ethnic minorities.

The newly-created and improved languages have been under careful experimentation and testing. So far, all the written languages are being experimentally practiced except for the Zhuang language and standard Yi language in Sichuan which have been approved by the State Council and officially put into use.

In June 1991, when approving the notice on the "Report on Strengthening the Work on Ethnic minority Languages from State Ethnic Affairs Commission," the State Council pointed out that, "for written languages created or improved in the 1950s, those welcomed by the majority shall be reported to be approved for implementation; those that did not achieve ideal results shall be further improved; and those that did not gain a good response from the majority shall not be forced upon to be implemented." This instruction fully indicated the

Kirgiz herdsmen are singing the national epic *Manas*.

complexity of the creation and reform of ethnic minority written languages.

Language equality has always served as an important symbol of China's ethnic policy. It is a belief of China's ethnic policy that there's no ethnic equality without language equality. In the National People's Congress of the People's Republic of China (NPC) and the Chinese People's Political Consultative Conference (CPPCC), translation and simultaneous interpretation in seven ethnic minority languages are provided for representatives and committee members of ethnic minorities, including the Mongol, Tibetan, Uygur, Kazak, Korean, Zhuang, and Yi minorities.

In the late 20th century, successive breakthroughs were made in China's ethnic minority language information processing system and electronic publishing system. Tibetan was China's first ethnic minority language with an international standard. In 1984, when DOS dominated computer operating systems, Northwest University for Nationalities began research on the "Tibetan language

Naxi ancient music of Lijiang in Yunnan is known as "the living fossil of Chinese music."

information processing system." In 1997, when the U.K., the U.S., India and other countries all proposed programs for Tibetan language code, the ISO voted to approve the Tibetan language code international standard with China's proposal. At the beginning of 1999, researchers in Zhongguancun completed the first Tibetan windows system, the first Tibetan language processing program, and the world's first Tibetan website after a whole year's hard work.

In fact, the information processing for the Tibetan language has achieved the same level as that for the language of the Han ethnic group. To date, with the promotion of the Chinese government, information processing and electronic publishing has become a reality for the written languages of 11 ethnic minorities, including Tibetan, Mongolian, Uygur, Kazakh, Kirgiz, Korean, Yi, Zhuang, Dai, Xibo and Manchu.

In the 21st century, cell phones in ethnic minority languages began to appear. The first ethnic minority language cell phone in Uygur appeared in January 2004. It had a Uygur menu and the function of writing Ugur SMS. Later, cell phones in Mongolian, Tibetan, Yi and other ethnic minority languages appeared one after another. In November 2007, a MMS mobile paper in Tibetan language was launched in Gansu Province, the first ethnic minority MMS mobile paper in China.

Press and publishing

The Ethnic Press of China was established in 1953 and it was an unusual press. Its name was inscribed by then Premier Zhou Enlai, and its president and editor-in-chief was Sa Kongliao who, at the same time was Deputy Head of the General Administration of Press and Publication (GAPP).

The Ethnic Press of China worked with some professional publishing houses soon after its foundation and published comic strips and maps in ethnic minority language, Uygur classical music *Twelve Mukams* and other ethnic minorities' books, filling in a series of gaps in the history of China's ethnic minorities' publications.

The Ethnic Press of China founded the *Nationality Pictorial* in 1955 and its name was once again written by Premier Zhou Enlai. It soon became one of the three most famous pictorials in China. *National Unity* magazine began publishing in 1957 and it was an exclusive magazine for ethnic minorities. After the 1980s, the *National Pictorial* and *National Unity* were published in five ethnic minority languages, including Tibetan, Uygur, Mongolian, Kazakh and Korean.

Xinjiang People's Publishing House and Mongolian People's Publishing House were established in 1951. Guangxi People's Publishing House was set up in 1952. Seven years later, Ningxia People's Publishing House was founded. And in 1971, Tibetan People's Publishing House was established. All these companies publish various books in the local ethnic minority language and Han language.

Meanwhile, in some provinces with multiple ethnic groups, compilation and translation bureaus for respective languages were gradually set up. Some autonomous regions also established publishing houses, mostly focusing on books in ethnic minority languages or having exclusive compilation and translation offices.

In the 1950s, provincial papers were published in succession in the five autonomous regions, among which the *Guangxi Daily* and *Ningxia Daily* were published in the Han language, while the other three were published both in the local ethnic minority language and Han language.

In the 21st century, China's news publishing faced massive reforms and changes—the marketization and commercialization of publishing. However, according to the plan of the State Press and Publication Administration, publication in ethnic minority languages is defined as "publication for public welfare." In other words, to ensure that the publication of ethnic minority languages may not be impacted by commercialization, all the ethnic minority language publication houses in China are entitled to publication subsidies from the government's financial expenditure.

No matter if it is in the past or present, no other country in the world could compare with China with respect to the operation, quantity and investment of news publishing houses and their range of publications.

Folk arts

Jiangbianjiacuo is a Tibetan who was born in Batang County, Sichuan Province. He was an interpreter for the 14th Dalai Lama and the 10th Penchan Lama in the early years after the People's Republic of China was founded. In 1981 he put aside his devoted translation and compilation career and started to research *Gesar*.

Starting from 1983, when the government formulated the Sixth Five-Year Plan (1981–1985), the Seventh Five-Year Plan (1986–1990), and the Eighth Five-Year Plan (1991–1995), the collection and research on *Gesar* was listed three times as a national key scientific research project. Jiangbianjiacuo was in charge of this project. During the Ninth Five-Year Plan (1996–2000), he finally began work on the compilation and publication of a selected edition of *Gesar*. The selected edition consists of 40 volumes, each containing 400, 000 words, totaling 16 million words. It was a huge cultural project.

The Chinese government sent research teams made up of hundreds of scholars and scientists to Tibet to do surveys on *Gesar*. The survey started from the 1950s and lasted for decades until today. "The searching and sorting task was the largest and the longest in Tibetan culture history that involved the largest number of people, achieved the greatest success and had the most extensive impact. It was an unprecedented feat in history," wrote Jiangbianjiacuo in his memoir.

For the research and transmission of *Gesar*, another great achievement was that the Tibetan version *Gesar* had been officially published in nearly 100 volumes after the foundation of the People's Republic of China, with a total of nearly 4 million copies, which meant that, according to the Tibetan population, each adult owned more than one copy of *Gesar*.

So far, *Gesar* has become one of the most dynamic fields of research in China's folk literature.

The *Twelve Mukàms* opera can be rated as the treasure in Uygur culture. However, due to the disruption of wars and social unrest, very few artists can perform the whole opera. Tuerdiahong, a master in his 70s, was the last person who could sing the whole opera in the 1950s.

In 1950, the Ministry of Culture of China sent music experts to Xinjiang to save the *Twelve Mukams*. Tuerdiahong sang the whole *Twelve Mukams* twice into a tape recorder. After the recording, the great folk artist passed away. One year later, the *Twelve Mukams Music Collection* was published.

After the People's Republic of China was founded, the government was committed to protecting and promoting the folk arts of ethnic minorities. As research for ethnic minorities' social history and language began in the 1950s, the government organized resources to search for and save folk arts. In the early 1980s, a huge publication project was launched, where up to 50,000 experts and cultural workers participated in this project. They spent 20 years compiling folk art materials collected during surveys into the "10 Collection and Annals of Chinese Ethnic/Folk Literature and Arts" (*Collection of Chinese Folk Songs, Collection of Chinese Folk Stories, Collection of Chinese Folk Proverbs, Collection of Chinese Folk Ballads, Collection of Chinese Local Operas Music, Collection of Chinese Quyi Music, Collection of Chinese Folk Dance, Collection of Chinese Folk Instrumental Music, Annals of Chinese Local Operas, and Annals of Chinese Quyi*). The collection, a complete record of the folk arts and literature data of the 56 ethnic groups was published in 310 volumes.

Ethnic study and collation of ancient works

Let every ethnic group have its own history book;

Let every ethnic language have its own brief record;

Let every autonomous region have its own overview record…

It was a magnificent and unprecedented publication blueprint.

A team of over 3,000 people wrote 401 books with over 80 million words in over a decade. It was an unprecedented writing and publishing project in the history of publishing both at home and abroad. It became a wonder in the world's publishing community as it had such a large scale, so many words and such complete data.

The program to compile the *Five Collections on Ethnic Issues* derived from voluminous precious materials obtained from social, historical and linguistic research on ethnic minorities in the 1950s. In 1964, based on first-hand data collected from social and history research, the Chinese Academy of Sciences compiled three collections: *The Brief History of Ethnic Minorities in China, A Brief Introduction to Chinese Ethnic Minorities,* and *An Overview of Chinese Ethnic Autonomous Regions.*

In 1978, the State Ethnic Affairs Commission pointed out that the *Three Collections* should continue to be compiled and expanded to *Five Collections on Ethnic Issues*; two collections were added: *Ethnic Minorities in China* (1 volume) and *The Collection of Social and historical Survey Data of Ethnic Minorities in China* (148 volumes).

Thirteen years later in October 1991, *Five Collections on Ethnic Issues* was published by 32 publishing houses. Four hundred and one kinds of books were issued in over 1.83 million volumes.

Five Collections on Ethnic Issues were a milestone in the study of Chinese ethnic issues. The value of this first-hand historical data has become more and more precious as time goes by.

A large-scale collation of ethnic minority ancient works began in 1984. In March of that year, the State Ethnic Affairs Commission submitted the "Request on Saving and Collating Ancient Works of Ethnic minorities" to the Central Government. It said, "According to incomplete statistics, there are over 10,000 ancient works of the Yi minority scattered around the country. There are over 10,000 kinds of ancient Tibetan works, and over 1,500 kinds of ancient Mongolian works. As for ancient Manchu works, there were over 1.5 million archive files, which is just the tip of the iceberg. All these ancient works had never been collated systematically before."

The State Council quickly released exclusive papers on this issue. The papers pointed out that ancient works of ethnic minorities are a part of China's precious cultural heritage. All local governments and departments shall provide enough manpower as well as financial and material support; they shall create good working conditions for people who are in charge of search and collation, and train talented people for ancient works collation and research.

In July 1984, the national planning team for the collation and publication of ancient works of ethnic minorities was founded.

The search and collation of ancient works of ethnic minorities started with "saving people." Written ancient works of some ethnic minorities were rarely handed down due to migration. Many ancient songs and ballads were passed down generation after generation orally and were able to remain to this day, thanks to the elderly artists who were still alive. Therefore, "saving people" became the first slogan of saving ancient works.

"Saving books" was the second slogan. A large volume of

lost ancient works were found and collected in the survey and were quickly collated and published.

To date, 120,000 (kinds, copies or volumes of) ancient books of ethnic minorities have been saved; 110,000 volumes of books have been collated. Over 5,000 kinds of ancient books of over 40 ethnic minorities have been published. Meanwhile, this campaign has also trained a group of excellent talented researchers for the study of ancient ethnic works.

Traditional sports

In the 1990s, Chinese sports experts surprisingly found that more than 1,000 folk sports were still being practiced in China till the end of the 20th century.

They were surprised, because after 100 years' spreading of Western sports concepts and models, Western sports have become the mainstream of Chinese sports. Therefore, it was unimaginable that traditional Chinese sports still existed in such a large scale.

Kazak traditional sport—horse racing.

Another figure gave experts a surprise as well. Among these 1,000 traditional sports, more than 700 of them originated from China's 55 ethnic minorities. This demonstrated that China has a rich variety of traditional sports, a large part of which were from ethnic minorities.

In fact, the diversity of ethnic minorities' traditional sports was respected and cherished by the Chinese government as early as the middle of 20th century. This was reflected in the National Sports Games for Ethnic Minorities, which have been held in China on a large scale since the 1950s. Till now, there have been eight sports games, and they are welcomed and appreciated by ethnic minorities. Many traditional sports on the verge of extinction survived because of these sports events.

Mongolian beloved sport - wrestling, is known as the Mongolian "three arts," together with horse racing and archery.

Besides the National Sports Games for Ethnic Minorities, sports games at the provincial level were also increasing. All provinces, municipalities and autonomous regions hold their own ethnic minority sports games on a regular basis.

In addition, the research and collection of ethnic minorities' traditional sports are underway. Some schools began offering traditional physical education courses of ethnic minorities.

The Protection of Intangible Cultural Heritages of Ethnic Minorities

In the 21st century, a movement for preserving intangible cultural heritage has evoked many people's emotions towards alienated traditional local culture.

The year 2003 was regarded as "the first year for the protection of China's intangible cultural heritage." At the beginning of the year, the Chinese folk culture protection project officially launched. This project will last until 2020, and a comparatively complete protection system of intangible cultural heritage will be established in China. The Ministry of Culture has established China's protection center for intangible cultural heritage. The second Saturday of each June was identified as Chinese Cultural Heritage Day. During the following years, "intangible cultural heritage" will become a frequently used word in Chinese society.

Till the end of 2008, the State Council has made public two lists of State-level intangible cultural heritage, totaling 1,028 items. Among these, the cultural heritage of ethnic minorities account for a significant proportion. In fact, because of geographical location and backward economy, more original cultural patterns are better preserved in some

Left: In Tongren County of Qinghai, a monk is drawing Thangka. Regong art is originated locally, including many art forms such as murals, Thangka, sculpture, Duixiu, and butter.

Right: An old man of the Li minority is weaving cotton by hand. The traditional textile dyeing and embroidery techniques of the Li minority have been listed in the United Nations' Urgent Safeguarding of Intangible Cultural Heritage.

ethnic minority areas than in Han areas, which made ethnic minority areas become the focus of protecting intangible cultural heritage. In the perspective of intangible culture heritage, ethnic minority culture has shaken off the label of "backwardness," and regained its magical charm.

The intangible culture heritage of ethnic minorities attracts more and more people's attention, and people are keen to experience it; meanwhile, these heritages have become national key protected objects. As for those listed at the national level, the government clearly states that preferential policies will be given to a protection fund and specialized guidance. From 2002 to 2008, one-quarter of the protection fund was used in ethnic minority areas, much higher than the population proportion of ethnic minorities in the whole country. In order to test the cultural integrity protection mode, China established four cultural and ecological preservation experimental zones, two of which are located

The Qiang watchtowers in Sichuan are regarded as a masterpiece of the Qiang minority's architectural art.

in ethnic minority areas—the Regong cultural and ecological preservation experimental zone and the Qiang cultural and ecological preservation experimental zone. The government has established a series of specialized museums, folk museums and education centers for intangible cultural heritage of ethnic minorities. In addition, experts and scholars began discussing the possibility of protecting traditional cultural heritage of minorities by legal means.

After the Wenchuan earthquake in 2008 in Sichuan Province, the Qiang minority, which is located in the earthquake epicenter and has a long history, became the concern of the whole society. Rescuing Qiang cultural relics and saving endangered Qiang intangible cultural heritage in the earthquake became a top priority in post-quake reconstruction.

This shows that in the era of globalization, culture, respected and concerned, has already been considered as the soul of a nation.

▶ Data Link

Protection of Intangible Cultural Heritages of Ethnic Minorities

Since 2002, the Chinese government has invested an accumulated fund of 386 million yuan into intangible cultural heritage protection, and about one-quarter of it is used in ethnic minority regions. Among the 1,028 items of national-level intangible cultural heritage identified by the State Council, 367 belong to ethnic minorities, accounting for 35.7 percent. All 55 ethnic minorities have their own enlisted budgets. Of the 1,488 representative inheritors of State-level intangible cultural heritage, 393 are from ethnic minorities, accounting for 26.4 percent. Ethnic minority culture heritage, such as Xinjiang Uygur Mukam art, Mongolian Long-tuned Songs, Dong Grand Song, Tibetan epic *Gesar*, Tibetan opera, Regong art, *Epic of Manas* of the Kirgiz minority, Chinese Korean farmers' music and dance, Mongolian Khoomei singing art, and Qinghai hua'er have been enlisted in the UN's "Representative List of Intangible Cultural Heritage of Mankind;" the Qiang minority's new year, and Li minority's traditional textile dyeing embroidery techniques were listed in the UN's "List of Intangible Cultural Heritage in Need of Urgent Safeguarding."

Industrialized Traditional Culture of Ethnic Minorities

Is it possible for the culture of ethnic minorities to be capitalized and industrialized? Of course!

In the 21st century, great changes have happened to the consumption structure and consumer psychology, and cultural consumption has become a popular mode. Against such a backdrop, the marketization, industrialization and commercialization of the cultures of ethnic minorities have taken hold.

In the past, some held the view that traditional ethnic culture hindered "modernization" which was a common aspiration of all people, since traditional culture showed great inconsistencies with modernization, and thus contradicted with modernization. For a long period, "modernization" and "ethnic traditional culture" were two dueling values in China, which stood for the contradiction between advanced and primitive, rich and poor.

With the ongoing reform and opening up, the paradox of modernization and traditional culture is changing. When the 21st century dawned, the two became surprisingly cooperative. The public begin to wonder how to convert traditional cultural advantages into economic advantages.

This is a dramatic change of Chinese ideas, where past obstacles of modernization have evolved into a very precious resource.

From confrontation to integration, the evolution is accompanied with the gradual progress of modernization with Chinese characteristics. The implementation of a market economy reveals the value of traditional culture, launching the country onto the road of modernization.

On this journey, ethnic minority culture is especially attractive because its original form is well-preserved. That creates many opportunities when it is exposed to the modern world.

First of all, traditional ethnic minority culture with distinctive features is transformed into a priceless tourism resource. Compared with other scenic spots, it does not only provide the tourists with natural landscapes, but also exotic cultural legacies, products, and also lifestyle. In the 21st century, ethnic customs and folk cultural legacies have become the driving force of tourism.

Secondly, many cultural activities are developed into products and put into the market. For example, the largest ethnic minority, the Zhuang minority, has a keen interest in folksongs. In the areas where many of the Zhuang minority are based, songfests often attract tens of thousands of people. In order to turn it into an economic booster, Guangxi Autonomous Region has decided to hold the "Guangxi International Folksong Festival," forging a commercial chain

Nanning International Folk Song Art Festival has become an icon of Guangxi in the world.

Old town of Lijiang in Yunnan is home to the Naxi people, as well as the desirable destination for tourists.

and developing a series of cultural products. Folksinging, an old cultural tradition, has become the engine of economic growth.

A case in point, Lijiang in Yunnan Province where the Naxi minority lives in compact communities, relies on ethnic culture to develop the local economy. The ancient city of Lijiang, full of Naxi flavor, has turned itself from a remote township into an international tourism destination, attracting millions of tourists from home and abroad each year. Tourism revenues account for half of the local gross domestic product (GDP).

Yunnan Province was once a forgotten place because of

its remote location and backward economy. However, since the 21st century, the home of 15 ethnic groups has suddenly caught the attention of the Chinese. It is considered a haven for tourists, and traveling to Yunan has become fashionable in many people's eyes. In fact, it is the strategic goal of Yunnan to build itself into an ethnic cultural province, to nurture new economic growth points by promoting the local cultural industry on the basis of local ethnic culture.

It is true that during this process, dramatic changes have happened to ethnic cultures. For example, as a post-modernist industry, tourism has a deconstructive effect on tourism destinations, decoupling traditional culture from social life, making ethnic culture become more like a souvenir or a commercial venture, and lose its original flavor. This has become a contentious issue.

Of course, this is an issue worldwide. In China, the idea of "cultural self-awareness," proposed by Fei Xiaotong, is a guideline for many scholars working on the above mentioned issue. In a cultural transition brought on by economic development, an ethnic group should take the initiative to make independent choices concerning its cultural development while adapting to new environments; maintain its original cultural characteristics and position itself well among world cultures.

This is what "cultural self-awareness" is about.

Modern Education for Ethnic Minorities in China

After appointed President of Central Academy of National Minorities in 1950, Ulanhu established the first institution of higher education for ethnic minorities.

At that time, the newly established People's Republic of China had numerous tasks to undertake. In spite of financial difficulties, the central government spared no effort to support the construction of the Central Academy of National Minorities. In less than two years, a new campus, designed by famous architect Liang Sicheng was presented to the public. It is a classical-looking compound with distinctive ethnic features: large roofs, grey bricks and black tiles, bricks with tight joints, painted beams and red columns, trees and flowers scattered around.

Over the next 50 years 15 institutions of higher education for ethnic minorities were established in China. Six of them are under the supervision of the State Ethnic Affairs Commission, namely, Minzu University of China, Southwest University for Nationalities, South-Central University for Nationalities, Northwest University for Nationalities, The North University for Ethnics, and Dalian Nationalities University. The remaining nine are under the administration of provincial governments, and they are: Inner Mongolia University for Nationalities, Guangxi University for Nationalities,

The highest institution of ethnic higher education in China—Minzu University of China.

Yunnan University of Nationalities, Qinghai University for Nationalities, Tibet Institute for Nationalities, Guizhou University for Nationalities, Hubei University for Nationalities, and Sichuan University for Nationalities.

All the above universities and colleges have developed multi-level diversified education models focusing on undergraduate education, supplemented by preparatory, graduate, doctorate, and post doctorate education, as well as cadre training. The latest surveys show that the number of students has exceeded 200,000 in these 15 ethnic universities and colleges.

Special educational policies

In China, the education of ethnic minorities is the fundamental way to improve the comprehensive quality and economic status of ethnic minorities.

In order to promote the education of ethnic minorities, the central government endorses autonomy in developing the education of ethnic minorities. The Constitution of the People's Republic of China stipulates that government organs in autonomous areas may decide their own local education programs, including the establishment of schools, the length of schooling, educational systems, forms, curricula, teaching languages, and procedures for enrollment.

Because of their relatively backward local economy, ethnic minorities may be financially incapable of developing their education. As early as the beginning of the People's Republic of China, the government set up a fund to subsidize the education of ethnic minorities. This is a fund that ethnic minority schools of various types and levels enjoy apart from subsidies that common schools also have, and the amount of this fund has continually increased in the past decades.

In the annual enrollment of colleges, universities and

polytechnic schools, favorable policies encourage to students from ethnic minorities to apply. Based on the various local situations in different provinces, autonomous regions and municipalities, these measures take the form of lowering admission scores, keeping certain quotas of candidates from ethnic minorities, setting separate admission scores, or making preferential enrollment policies for these ethnic minorities with small populations.

All schools in China are open to both students of the Han ethnic group and ethnic minorities. However, many local governments have opened ethnic schools for students of ethnic minorities, or set up ethnic classes for ethnic minority students in common schools.

Ethnic schools refer to educational institutions that mainly enroll students from ethnic minorities, including high schools, primary schools as well as vocational schools. It is either founded by a single ethnic minority or co-established by two or more ethnic minorities. The aim of ethnic schools is not to differentiate the ethnicity of

In an ethnic school in Xijiang, teachers and students are at class.

students. The government gives priority to them in terms of staff and facilities, and ensures the education of ethnic minority languages at the same time.

Ethnic classes are a sort of special education which is similar to common schools in terms of teachers and facilities, but only enroll students of ethnic minorities. Facing the fact that there was still a low proportion of students from ethnic minorities enrolled even after lowering the admission scores for them, in 1980, the Ministry of Education decided to open ethnic classes in the five universities under its direct administration. Afterwards, ethnic classes appeared in some medical colleges, institutes of water conservancy and hydroelectric power, as well as institutes of physical education. In 1984, documents were released by the Ministry of Education and Committee of State Ethnic Affairs, which specified the regulations on enrollment, placement of graduates, courses, and administrative management, of ethnic classes, making this educational form more mature and practical. Since then, ethnic classes were opened in key middle schools, vocational

Mongolian children are playing at school.

schools and schools for adult education.

Ethnic classes in primary and middle schools were established for students in places where there are no ethnic schools. Only students of ethnic minorities can attend ethnic classes. Those attendees in ethnic classes are eligible for scholarships, tuition exemption or reduction, and subsidies will be given to students in very poor financial situations. Most students of ethnic classes eat in school cafeterias and are given the same treatment as those attending boarding schools.

The Daur students are having a computer class.

Boarding schools are an effective measure by the Chinese government to improve the educational conditions of ethnic minorities. The Law of the People's Republic of China on Ethnic Regional Autonomy clearly stipulates that public ethnic primary and middle schools that provide boarding and allowances to most students are established in pastureland and mountainous regions where families mostly have financial difficulties and live in scattered locations. In practice, autunomous governments at all levels shall open ethnic primary and middle schools that provide boarding to students in sparsely populated areas with poor traffic services, especially in prairie and nomadic regions. All the costs for the construction of these schools shall be assumed by provincial, municipal and county governments and by the central government through preferential treatment in terms of funding, staff and facilities. Students in boarding schools are eligible for scholarships, tuition exemption and subsidies. Until now, there are 6,000 primary and middle boarding schools in China.

Preparatory education for ethnic minorities is a unique development in China. As a special phase in higher education, it serves as a transition period for students enrolled into universities through preferential policies. It works like this: in normal or ethnic minority universities, preparatory courses are run especially for ethnic minority students. These are tailor-made complimentary courses for students with poor academic backgrounds.

Since the 1950s, preparatory programs have been offered in many technical secondary schools and institutions of higher education. Preparatory education has become part of the ethnic education system and a shortcut to speed up the educational progress. Usually, preparatory programs are a year long; they may be prolonged to two if the students have a poorer command of Chinese. After finishing the courses, ethnic minority students who have passed the examinations go directly to universities or colleges for further education.

Bilingual education

As stipulated in the Law of the People's Republic of China on Regional National Autonomy, bilingual education is a basic educational system practiced among schools in ethnic regions. It means school lessons are given in both local native languages and Chinese for those students in places where ethnic minorities concentrated, and have their own spoken and written languages. This system, based on local situations, caters to the will of ethnic minorities.

Considering the different language environments and statuses of written languages among different ethnic minorities in various regions, native language education and bilingual education are mainly divided into three types:

(1) Schools in areas where ethnic minorities have spoken languages but no written languages and Chinese is the

Ethnic students in Yunnan are having a class of mandarin phonetics.

commonly used language; courses are given in both Chinese and native tongue, but not run courses for native languages.

(2) For ethnic minorities who have widely spoken and written languages, courses are taught in both Chinese and native tongue. Schools run both local language and Chinese courses, and emphasize the aquisition and application of ethnic languages.

(3) For ethnic minorities who have their own spoken and written languages but use Chinese more often, courses are taught in both Chinese and native tongue. Schools run courses both for local languages and Chinese, and emphasize the aquisition and application of Chinese.

The country has been very supportive of bilingual education. For example, favorable financial measures have been taken to improve the editing, translating, proofing and publishing of textbooks in ethnic minority languages.

At present, bilingual education is carried out in over 10,000 schools in 13 provinces and autonomous regions in the country. In those schools, there are 6 million ethnic minority students from 21 ethnic groups, involving 60 ethnic minority languages in total.

The Economy of Ethnic Minorities in China

Are There Any Independent Ethnic Minority Economies?

In March 197,9 nobody was skeptical when "Economics of Chinese Ethnic Minorities" was listed as 27th among the 30 disciplines for scientific development planning of the national economy. In the initial stage of reform and opening up, people found it urgent to establish a discipline studying the economic development of ethnic minorities and ethnic regions.

However, by the end of the 1980s, with the all-round and in-depth development of the market economy in China, one doubt began to surface: in a market economy, are there still any independent ethnic minority economies or ethnic regional economies?

The development of a market economy leaps over the

Tourism characterized by grassland scenery and ethnic customs has become one of the important economic sectors in Inner Mongolia.

boundaries between various closed economic systems that were caused by the planned economy in China. Thus, regional economies once divided by administrative units, geographic units or communities all gradually disappeared in the country.

In a market economy, economies once divided by administrative units, such as Guangxi, Inner Mongolia and Xinjiang, and economies divided by communities, such as the Hui minority and Tibetan minority have seen the gradual disappearance of their relative isolation and independence. Under the law of value in a market economy, through the optimal allocation of production factors and resources, all parts of the country, including ethnic autonomous areas, as well as China's 56 ethnic groups, are closely linked and inseparable.

The socialist market economy with Chinese characteristics has greatly changed the traditional economic system of ethnic minorities in China, forming a new pattern of economic development, raising the level of economic development of ethnic groups and improving the living standards of 55 ethnic minorities.

Although relatively independent ethnic regional economies or ethnic minority economies in planned economy are no longer the subject matter of research, the economics of ethnic groups has broadened its study fields, made great achievements, and established an innovative theoretical system in domains such as the gap between east and west China, sustainable development of ethnic regions, development of acceleration strategies, human resources development in western China, the ecosystem in western China, opening up borders and border trade, and the urbanization of ethnic regions and rural economy.

Thus far, a development system of talent concerning the economics of ethnic groups has been established in 30 higher educational institutions for undergraduates, masters, doctorates and post-doctorates in China. From 1994 and 2002, there were 6,200 research papers on the economics of ethnic groups published in well-known domestic academic periodicals. The growth of this discipline reflects the active, dynamic and continuous changes of Chinese ethnic minority economies in the last three decades.

The Transition of Traditional Economy

Before the founding of the People's Republic of China, ethnic minorities were mainly engaged in traditional farming and animal husbandry: some regions were still in the state of "slash and burn;" iron tools had not been widely used; and there were still people using implements made of wood or stone in some areas.

However, in the second half of the 20th century, traditional economies of Chinese ethnic minorities generally finished

The nomads of China are mainly in the northern and northwestern regions, and most of them have already settled down.

their transitions in varying degrees.

The Oroqen minority and Ewenki minority in northeast China once lived mainly by hunting and gathering; and the Hezhen minority mainly sustained themselves by fishing. After the founding of the People's Republic of China, with the guidance and help of the government, the Oroqen minority and Ewenki minority completed their gradual transition to settled farming; in the 1990s, the Hezhen minority also bid farewell to fishing and hunting, and began farming. Owing to the tourism potential of the Hezhen minority's fishing and hunting culture, with the help of the local government, tourism related to fishing and hunting has now developed into a leading

In the countryside of Yunnan, ethnic minority people are working on the farm.

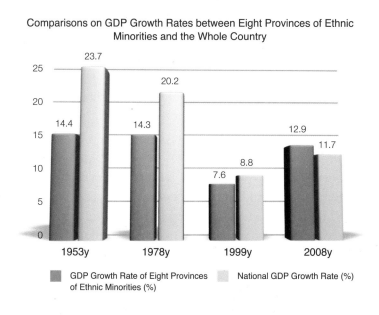

Comparisons on GDP Growth Rates between Eight Provinces of Ethnic Minorities and the Whole Country

GDP Growth Rate of Eight Provinces of Ethnic Minorities (%)

National GDP Growth Rate (%)

industry in regions inhabited by the Hezhen minority.

Ethnic groups in the north and west of China used to live nomadic lives, such as the Mongol minority, Tibetan minority, Kazak minority, Kirgiz minority, Yugur minority, and Tajik minority. Ever since the 1950s, the Chinese government has encouraged settled grazing instead of the nomadic life, called for the combination of farming and animal husbandry, as well as sideline production such as processing animal products. Nowadays, these ethnic groups are no longer pure herdsmen. They are engaged in agricultural production and cash crops planting, as they continue with grazing; villages and towns have emerged in previously nomadic regions.

Ethnic groups in the south and southwest of China, such as the She minority, Va minority, Lahu minority, Lisu minority, and Nu minority, generally adopted the "slash and burn" mode of production before the founding of the PRC; but since receiving organization from the government, these ethnic groups have adopted settled farming.

Generally speaking, the level of economic development of certain ethnic minorities who live together with the Han ethnic group or live near regions inhabited by the Han ethnic group in compact communities, have basically reached or approached the economic level of the Han ethnic group, such as the Zhuang minority, Hui minority, Manchu minority, and Korean minority. For more than half a century, the economic development in these ethnic regions is basically in line with the Han region: from traditional agriculture to modern intensive agriculture; a large-scale development of modern industry and commodity economy.

To briefly sum up the changes of Chinese ethnic minority economies over the past half century, these economies have gradually transformed themselves from a natural economy to a commodity economy.

Supportive Policies of the Government

In 1995, the total fiscal revenue of ethnic autonomous regions in China reached 30.8 billion yuan, while the total fiscal expenditure was 74.6 billion yuan;

In 2006, the total fiscal revenue of ethnic autonomous regions in China was 128 billion yuan, while the total fiscal expenditure reached 373.4 billion RMB.

These two sets of figures show the tremendous economic growth of ethnic autonomous regions in China and at the same time raises a question: between the fiscal revenue and expenditure in Chinese ethnic autonomous regions, there was a huge gap, which was 43.8 billion yuan in 1995 and as much as 245.4 billion yuan in 2006.

Who filled this huge gap? State finance!

After the founding of the PRC, the fiscal expenditure of ethnic autonomous regions in China has been relying on subsidies from the State and local finance at the provincial

Silk factory in Hotan, Xinjiang.

Manchuria port of Inner Mongolia is the largest land port in China, serving as a distributing center of a large number of import and export goods.

level. According to incomplete statistics, from 1959 to 2008 (Tibet carried out democratic reform in 1959), financial aid provided by the central government to Tibet added up to 201.9 billion yuan, with an average annual growth rate of nearly 12 percent; from 1955 to 2008 (Xinjiang Uygur Autonomous Region was established in 1955), financial aids provided by the central government to Xinjiang totaled 375.2 billion yuan, with an average annual growth rate of 11 percent.

Judging from the financial aid policy, we can get a clear picture of the policy that the Chinese government has pursued consistently concerning the economic development of ethnic minorities and ethnic regions: vigorously supporting, narrowing the gap, and achieving common prosperity.

As early as the 1960s, the Chinese government implemented the Three Financial Aid policies in ethnic autonomous regions. They are firstly, an extra 5 percent emergency fund is added to fiscal expenditure budget in ethnic autonomous regions; secondly, the proportion of financial reserve in ethnic autonomous regions is higher than that in other regions; thirdly, an annual subsidy is provided to ethnic minority regions for certain special expenditures.

After the 1990s, besides fixed quotas for financial subsidies, China has established some special subsidies to support the development of various undertakings in ethnic regions. For instance, education subsidies for border areas and ethnic minority regions, border construction subsidies, funds for supporting the development of underdeveloped regions, and funds earmarked for construction in Tibet.

With regard to taxation, ethnic autonomous regions are endowed with a certain degree of decision-making power in terms of tax reduction. The provincial governments in ethnic autonomous regions are entitled to reduce local taxes included in local financial revenues. Meanwhile, the government has carried out some policies of moderate tax reduction in ethnic regions. For example, the government has reduced the tax on enterprises in ethnic regions and manufacturers of ethnic minority products.

As for finance, the central government has set up special loans for ethnic regions, offering favorable interest rates, easing lending restrictions and repayment periods. For example, the government had established special trade subsidies in ethnic regions and special poverty discount loans for pastureland.

With regards to investment, China has formulated preferential policies to guide and encourage foreign and domestic investment in ethnic autonomous regions, giving priority to reasonable arrangements of resource development projects and infrastructure construction projects in ethnic autonomous regions. For more than half a century, a number of key projects were built in succession, such as the Sichuan-Tibet

Highway, Qinghai-Tibet Highway, Lan-Xin Railway, Qinghai-Tibet Railway, Lhasa Airport, Lan-Xining-Lhasa Optical Cable Engineering, and Ningxia Yellow River Pumping Project, which have greatly improved local infrastructure, such as transportation and communication, as well as production and living conditions in ethnic regions. The establishment of large industrial enterprises has also transformed ethnic regions into several industrial bases for resource exploration and resource further processing, such as the iron and steel base in Baotou of Inner Mongolia, Karamay Oilfield in Xinjiang, Tin Corporation in Gejiu of Yunnan, Tarim Oilfield in Xinjiang, Potash fertilizer project in Qinghai, and large-sized coal bases in Inner Mongolia.

In the exploitation of natural resources in ethnic regions, autonomous agencies in ethnic autonomous areas are permitted to rationally explore and use available local resources; and the country will financially compensate these ethnic autonomous regions that produce natural resources. Coal-mines, electricity plants, and forestry enterprises established by the central government in ethnic autonomous areas will be entitled to a proportion of the profits and products.

The War against Poverty

Before 1949 most ethnic minorities in China lived a hard life, especially those living in mountain areas and deserts, where food and clothes were in short supply, and even no food available for several months of every year. People there could only eat wild fruits and wear straw or palm-bark raincoats to protect themselves against the cold weather.

For years, the Chinese government has formulated a series of anti-poverty measures for ethnic minorities, including granting loans and distributing farm tools to the poor in ethnic minority regions, providing free medical services, opening public schools, and offering social aids. By 1985, there was still a poor population of over 40 million in ethnic regions.

In 1986 China declared war against poverty in the country and launched a planned, organized and extensive

Tibetan farmers are harvesting wheat.

Tianshan Mountain Ranch in Xinjiang.

development-oriented poverty relief scheme. At that time, there were 125 million people living in poverty with a poverty rate of 14.8 percent. Two decades later, or by 2006, the number of people living in poverty has dropped to 2.165 million, with a lower poverty rate of 2.5 percent.

Half of the poor population in China is made up of ethnic minorities. They mainly live in the Karst areas in the southwest, frigid and damp areas in the northwest, desert steppe in the northwest, and arid mountainous areas in the northwest. The harsh natural environments have become the biggest obstacle in the war against poverty.

The Karst area in the northwest of Guangxi Zhuang Autonomous Region covers an area of 89,000 square kilometers with extremely barren soil. More than 85 percent of poverty-stricken people in Guangxi live here and they are almost all from the Zhuang, Yao and Miao minorities. A report describes the life here as follows: the people here once channeled water droplets from high rock crevices into water vats at the foot of mountains through an iron wire; the corn plant grown in rock crevices was only 1 meter high and the corn was no bigger than a human fist.

The poverty relief in Guangxi was considered "a 20-year war in Karst hilly areas." In the mid 1980s, there were 15 million poor people in the rural areas of Guangxi. By 2004, there were only 840,000 people without enough food and clothing in Guangxi. The figures show that about 14 million people have been lifted out of poverty due to the long and painstaking "war" in the past 20 years.

In the war against poverty, the country is always paying ethnic regions unremitting attention. Ethnic minority regions enjoy a comparatively flexible standard, when the country identifies key poor-stricken areas to give special aid. As for poverty relief investment in capital and goods, ethnic minority regions also benefit in more allocations than other regions.

● Data Link

The Poverty Relief and Development of Ethnic Autonomous Areas

Among the 331 impoverished counties designated as key recipients of state aid in 1986, 141 are in ethnic autonomous areas, accounting for 42.6 percent of the total. In 1994 the State began implementing the Seven-Year Program for Delivering 80 Million People out of Poverty, and among the 592 impoverished counties designated as key recipients of state aid, 257 are in ethnic autonomous areas, accounting for 43.4 percent of the total. The Outline Program for Poverty Alleviation and Development in the Rural Areas of China, which began being implemented in 2001, once again recognized ethnic minority areas as key targets for assistance. In the 592 counties newly designated for state poverty alleviation and development, 267 are located in ethnic autonomous areas (excluding Tibet), accounting for 45.1 percent of the total. Tibet as a whole has been included as a target for key poverty alleviation and development from the state.

In addition, the government has set up a special fund for development and poverty relief for ethnic minorities.

Education, intellectual development, science and technology poverty relief schemes, for the purpose of improving the quality of poverty-stricken people, are regarded as the trump card in winning the anti-poverty war.

By 2008, the number of poor people living in ethnic regions in China was down to 7.7million. In 2009, China adopted a new standard for poverty relief and fully implemented the anti-poverty policy in all low-income populations in rural areas of ethnic regions.

Ethnic Trade

China's ethnic trade policy is unique in the world.

The so-called "ethnic trade" is a form of commodity trade in which the Chinese government adopts special supportive policies in accordance with the characteristics of ethnic regions.

In the early years of the PRC, commodity trade in ethnic regions showed two striking observations, to which the government attached great importance: first, many ethnic minorities lived in mountain areas, highland and grassland, with poor transport facilities, and goods were in a slow circulation due to transport difficulties, resulting in low efficiency in commodity trade enterprises; second, because all ethnic groups demanded commodities closely related to traditional culture, customs and faith, and so many ethnic groups showed special needs for certain commodities. For instance, there is a high demand for silver by the Miao, Yao and Dong minorities because of their unique clothing tradition; the Tibetan minority's love for tea; the special needs for Mongolian bowls and knives in Inner Mongolia; and the need for Muslim food in Islamic areas... The special attention given to the two unique observations fostered the establishment of an ethnic trade policy system by the Chinese government for the following few decades.

Muslim groceries in the streets of Shanghai.

The first national ethnic trade conference was held in August 1951. Chen Yun, then vice-premier of the Government Administration Council, declared at the conference for people not to ever regard ethnic trade simply as trading; ethnic trade is the concrete embodiment of ethnic policies; and people working in ethnic trade are those who implemented and enforced ethnic policies.

By 1963, five nationwide conferences had been held on ethnic trade. Just in that year, the concept of "three preferential policies for ethnic trade" officially emerged. The three aid policies were: "profit retention"—ethnic trade enterprises could retain 80 percent of the total profits, 30 percentage points higher than general enterprises; "self-owned funds"—wholesale enterprises had 50 percent self-owned funds, while retail enterprises had 80 percent, and local or state finance would make up the remainder. The government offered price subsidies in various forms to ethnic trade enterprises when they purchased farm and sideline products and sold daily industrial products, and gave freight subsidies to enterprises that delivered goods to remote places.

With the promotion of the market economy in China, ethnic trade policy has, after several important revisions, become a new policy system in line with the socialist market economy. In terms of content, the new preferential policy for ethnic trade includes finance, banking, taxation, and industry; as for means of support, it includes earmarked allocations, discounted loans, tax reduction, favorable interest rates and guidance for industry; its beneficiaries include ethnic trade enterprises in ethnic trade counties, ethnic trade corporations at provincial and prefecture levels, and designated manufacturers of ethnic commodities specially in demand; as for the distribution of sectors benefited, they are clothing, industrial arts, ethnic minority medicine, Muslim food, tea sold in border areas, publications in ethnic languages, folk musical instruments, and sports requisites for ethnic minorities, with all aspects of production and living involved.

The long-term national support to ethnic trade and ethnic commodities specially in need has lowered production and operation costs, strengthened market competitiveness and promoted commodity circulation and market prosperity in ethnic minority regions.

Western Development of China

Since 1999, "Western Development" has frequently appeared in Chinese society.

Since China's reform and opening up, regional development strategies have basically gone through four stages: giving priority to the eastern coastal areas; coordinating the development of east China and west China; attaching importance to and supporting the development of the central and western part of China; and implementing the Western Development Strategy.

The gap between east China and west China in economic development is both a long-standing issue in history and an issue of overall significance for social development in China. To achieve the coordinated development of east China and west China is an important strategic decision for the country in the 21st century.

Nearly 70 percent of the ethnic minority population lives in the west of China; ethnic minority regions cover three-quarters of the western areas, and one-third of the population are ethnic minorities. Therefore, Western Development proposed in 1999 is closely related to the economic development of ethnic regions. The CPC Central Committee clarified that the implementation of the Western Development strategy was aimed at accelerating the economic development of ethnic minorities and ethnic regions.

Strictly speaking, Inner Mongolia Autonomous Region and Guangxi Zhuang Autonomous Region do not belong to the western part of China from a geographical point of view; however, they are included in the scope of Western Development. Moreover, Yanbian Korean Autonomous Prefecture in the northeast, Enshi Tujia and Miao Autonomous Prefecture in Hubei Province, as well as Xiangxi Tujia and Miao Autonomous Prefecture in Hunan Province, which are

not geographically located in the west of China, are also in-cluded in this preferential policy.

In 2000 China made substantial progress in developing the western regions in China. The newly started Ten Projects focused on infrastructure construction to improve transpor-tation and the electrical power system in west China. In the interests of ethnic minorities and ethnic regions in Western Development, the country took many preferential measures, including giving priority to the exploitation and further pro-cessing of resources in ethnic regions, compensating those ethnic autonomous areas that produce natural resources, guiding and encouraging enterprises in developed areas to invest in ethnic regions, and increasing financial investment and financial support in ethnic regions.

Qinghai-Tibet Railway starts from Golmud of Qinghai (the east side) to Lhasa of Tibet (the west side), which was put into function in July 2006.

Karamay oilfield in Xinjiang is an important petrochemical base in western China.

Wind energy is made full use of in Inner Mongolia to develop "green energy."

Since the implementation of Western Development, a number of key projects have been completed, such as the West-East Natural Gas Transmission Project and West-East Power Transmission Project, and infrastructure have been built, such as airports, highways and hydro junctions, all of which have created better conditions for development in ethnic minority regions. In 2006 the Qinghai-Tibet Railway was open to traffic. This highest railway in the world ended the history of Tibet not having railways, and built an economical and fast transportation channel between Tibet and inland cities.

By 2008, the investment in fixed assets in ethnic regions has amounted to 7.7899 trillion yuan since the implementation of Western Development.

The western areas are the source of large rivers in China, and so the ecosystem is very fragile here. Therefore, the major tasks of Western Development also include containing the deterioration of the ecosystem in west China, improving the eco-environment and promoting environmental protection.

Fixed Assets Investment in Ethnic Regions after Western Development
(unit: 100 million yuan)

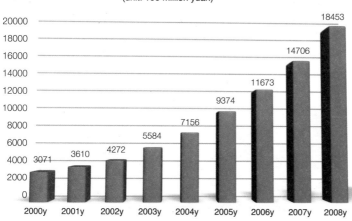

Paired-up Assistance

Paired-up assistance is a unique feature in China. It is a kind of practice led and organized by the Chinese government where developed inland provinces and cities help targeted underdeveloped areas with their social and economic development.

In 1979, the country made a list of paired-up areas: Beijing would assist Inner Mongolia, Hebei to help out Guizhou, Jiangsu to assist Guangxi and Xinjiang, Shandong to help out Qinghai, Shanghai to land a hand to Yunnan and Ningxia, and finally the whole nation to assist Tibet.

This list includes five ethnic minority autonomous regions and three provinces with a larger proportion of the ethnic minority population—Yunnan, Guizhou and Qinghai.

Tibet is the focus of national support. In 1984, the CPC Central Committee decided to implement "projects with state direct investment, financial subsidies from the central government, nationwide paired-up assistance to Tibet," which stated that nine comparatively developed provinces

A large number of winter supplies for Tibetans are transported by air to Gonggar Airport in Lhasa from the mainland.

and cities together with several ministries and commissions would help Tibet with the construction of 43 small and medium-sized projects closely related to people's livelihood. And the total investment reached nearly 500 million yuan.

In 1994, an upsurge in "nationwide support for Tibet" began in China. From 1994 to 2001, 15 provinces offering paired-up assistance together with central ministries and commissions, providing free aid for the construction of 716 projects. The annual GDP growth rate of Tibetan Autonomous Region reached 11.9 percent over the same period, higher than the national average for many years; a vast majority of poverty-stricken people solved the problem of food and clothing, and some even began to live a relatively comfortable life.

Engineering machinery and equipments transported from the mainland to Xinjiang.

In 2001, the country once again made the decision of prolonging the paired-up assistance to Tibet program for another 10 years, and the remaining 29 counties without paired-up assistance would be included into this practice in different ways; and the country should bear the expenses for the construction of key projects in Tibet.

○ Data Link

The Economic Development of Ethnic Regions in Figures

In 2008, the economic aggregate of ethnic regions increased from 5.79 billion yuan in 1952 to 3.06062 trillion yuan, with an increase of 92.5 times according to comparable prices. The per capita disposable income of urban population increased to 13,170 yuan, which was over 30 times more than that in 1978 (307 yuan); the per capita net income of farmers and herdsmen went up to 3,389 yuan, which was 20 times more than that in 1978 (138 yuan). The economic growth rate of Inner Mongolia ranks first in the country for seven consecutive years; Xinjiang has maintained a double-digit economic growth rate for six years; the total output value of Tibet in 2008 reached 39.591 billion yuan, which was 66 times more than that in 1959.

Religious Beliefs of
Chinese People

Don't the Chinese Have Any Religious Beliefs?

Chinese media once reported that Africans had an impression that Chinese people did not have religious beliefs. In Africa, when people go to government offices for certain matters, they need to fill in a series of forms, one of which is about religious beliefs. Chinese people working in Africa always leave empty the category of religion. Therefore, Africans were puzzled: how could people not have any religious beliefs? And what makes Africans even more curious was that Chinese people work on Sundays instead of going to church.

Don't Chinese people have any religious beliefs? As for this question, historical knowledge would be of great help.

In many parts of the world, people always associate China with Confucius. The sage is almost the representative of Chinese culture. Indeed this philosopher, who lived more than 2,500 years ago, had a great impact on Chinese culture with his doctrines. In a sense, Chinese people's lives are the

Lingyin Temple in Hangzhou of Zhejiang with numerous pilgrims.

product of Confucian culture.

Confucian culture holds a rational attitude towards society and life and focuses on politics, ethics and moral standards in practice. It believes that human rationality is the cornerstone of people's happiness and that the pursuit of a moral life leads to the transcendence of life. Thus, Confucian culture does not pursue fantasy happiness.

How does Western culture look at Confucian culture? As early as the 16th and 17th centuries, Confucian philosophy shed new light on the philosophers in the Enlightenment period in Europe. Gottfriend Wilhelm Le (1646–1716), an encyclopedic genius, argued that Confucian ethics was based on human rationality, and that China was almost an "ideal state," which had more or less realized Plato's "ideal state." Another great French philosopher Voltaire (1694–1778) also advocated Confucian culture. He once wrote, "It is ethics and law that Chinese people, taught by Confucius, understand best, nurture with utmost care and devote all their time and energy to... the ever happiest and most adorable time in the

Left: Pilgrims on Tibetan plateau.

Right: A Taoist is burning incense.

world is when people followed Confucius' laws."

Interestingly enough, although Confucian culture did not pursue dreamland happiness, it later developed into a religious system called Confucianism. But it is still an issue hotly debated over whether there is a "Confucian religion" in China. However, in China there is indeed a statement that "Confucianism, Buddhism, Taoism" are regarded as "three religions." In China, people once considered *Four Books* and *Five Classics* to be Confucian classics, and regarded the worship of ancestors and Confucius as prescribed rituals. As a matter of fact, Confucian philosophy in essence is knowledge of life. It is a combination of seeking enlightenment and obtaining knowledge, which solves not only questions in belief but also in knowledge; thus it is a philosophy as well as a religion.

In the countryside of Yunan, Catholics are praying in a church.

Ancient China experienced a special process of cultural development which was independent of the history of Western thought. As for religion, it may not work to simply take a set of Western concepts into china. Chinese culture has its own uniqueness.

Religious Beliefs in China

The massive influence that Confucian culture and Confucianismexerted on China does not indicate that Chinese people do not have any religions. In fact, there are five major religions in China. In addition, countless folk beliefs also exist in China.

Buddhism, introduced to China from India in the 1st century AD, has become the largest religion in China. Currently, China has more than 13,000 Buddhist temples with some

200,000 monks and nuns. Since there is no strict ceremony when one becomes a religious believer, it is difficult to get the exact number of Buddhists. According to the statistics issued by the national organization of Buddhism in China, the Buddhist Association of China, the country has about 100 million Buddhists.

Muslims are worshipping in Dongguan Muslim temple in Xining.

Taoism is a local religion that was formed in the 2nd century AD based on the ancient philosophy of Tao in China. There are more than 1,500 Taoist temples nationwide with 25,000 Taoist priests and nuns. It's also difficult to know the actual number of its followers since Taoism, like Buddhism, doesn't have strict admittance rites.

Islam entered China in the 7th century. Muslims are mainly distributed in 10 ethnic minorities. Scholars usually take for reference the total population of these 10 ethnic minorities, which amounts to 20 million, when they want to figure out

A Christian
church in Harbin,
Heilongjiang.

the total number of Muslims in China.

Catholicism was introduced into China in the 13th century and experienced ups and downs till the 1940s, when scores of Catholic missionaries rushed into China. Now the country is home to over 5 million Catholics with more than 5,000 churches and venues.

Christianity (referred to Protestantism in particular) made its way into China in 1807. By 2002, there were 16 million Christianity believers and 8,000 Protestant Churches in China.

Many Han people are religious believers, but they only account for less than 10 percent of the total population of religious believers in China. Chinese ethnic minorities have a large proportion of religious believers with deep faith. According to data, religious believers account for over 50 percent of the total population in 55 ethnic minorities. In over 20 ethnic minorities, every one used to be a religious believer in history, and currently religious believers still take a majority in these ethnic groups.

An Introduction to Five Major Religions

Buddhism

Chinese Buddhism

In 64 AD, guided by a magical dream, Emperor Ming of the Eastern Han Dynasty (reigned 58–75 AD) sent envoys to the Western Regions for Buddhist doctrines. Three years later, envoys returned to the capital Luoyang with two Indian Buddhist monks, and brought back Buddhist scriptures and Buddhist statues. The White Horse Temple was specially built near Luoyang by Emperor Ming, where Buddhist monks could settle down and translate Buddhist scriptures. The White Horse Temple is the first Buddhist temple in China and still exists to this day.

After entering China, Buddhism experienced a long period of interaction with two Chinese major schools of thoughts—Confucianism and Taoism. By the 7th century AD,

Buddhist activities in Tanzhesi Temple,Beijing.

Huineng (638–713), a Buddhist monk, founded Chinese Zen Buddhism based on traditional Chinese culture, and sinicized Buddhism in aspects of mind and doctrine, self-cultivation, and attainment of Buddhahood. Zen Buddhism's formation marked the complete sinicization of Buddhism in China.

Today, few Chinese people point out that Buddhism is a foreign culture for China. In fact, over the past 2,000 years, Buddhism has merged into Chinese culture. The acceptance and localization of Buddhism by Chinese culture should be a classic example of cultural integration in human history.

Buddhist culture in China has created many world-class cultural landscapes. There are three famous grottoes in the north of China: the Dunhuang Grottoes excavated in the 4th century AD, Yungang Grottoes and Longman Grottoes in the 5th century AD. These three grottoes have been listed by UNESCO on the "World Heritage List." The Dazu Rock Carvings in Chongqing are also on the list. It was excavated in the 9th century AD and was completed 250 years later.

In China, there are corresponding Buddhist sites for the four Bodhisattvas who represent great compassion, great wisdom, great vow and great practice. These are the four famous Buddhist mountains of China. Putuo Mountain in Zhejiang is the Buddhist site of Guanyin Bodhisattva with great compassion; Wutai Mountain in Shanxi is the Buddhist site of Manjusri Bodhisattva with boundless wisdom; Jiuhua Mountain in Anhui is the Buddhist site of Ksitigarbha Bodhisattva, who claimed that, "Not until all the hells are emptied will I become a Buddha;" Emei Mountain in Sichuan is the Buddhist site of Puxian Bodhisattva with great courage and practice. Many Buddhists in China regard pilgrimages to the four famous mountains as their most sacred wish.

According to the principle of selecting and appointing capable persons in contemporary temple management systems in China, based on democratic consultation, Buddhist monks in a temple elect an abbot to be in charge of the management of temple affairs. The tenure of the abbot is three years and the abbot can be re-elected. Monks are required to be dressed in monastic habit, eat a vegetarian diet, not marry, and strictly follow religious disciplines and Buddhist etiquette. Buddhist monks should chant Buddhist scriptures in the morning and evening, learn scriptures by memory, and keep practicing Buddhist rules.

Shaolin Temple may be the most influential Chinese temple overseas. When speaking of Chinese kungfu, everyone brings up Shaolin Temple. This ancient temple was built in 495 AD, which has become a symbol of Chinese martial arts. As the cradle of the Chinese Zen Buddhism, at the initial stage of its establishment, Shaolin Temple accepted Chinese martial arts as part of the monks' daily life and included it as part of scripture learning and self-cultivation. Fighting and developing in martial arts is an extreme form, since Buddhism advocates peace. Even in this extreme form, however, Chinese Zen Buddhism founded the innate philosophy that no extreme will hold long. It discovered the combination of dynamic extreme and static extreme, and the paramount truth beyond fighting and universal fraternity—the most contradictory thing for philosophy to transcend contradiction. This can be regarded as the mysterious great wisdom of Buddhism in China.

Since the 1980s, China has experienced an unprecedented upsurge in Buddhism. It is difficult to get an accurate number of Buddhists, but obviously more pilgrims are going to Buddhist temples and more incense is presented, so we can make an easy guess as to how fast the population of Buddhists is growing in China at present.

The Chinese government has a positive attitude towards the development of Buddhism. China has held two World

Buddhist Forums of unprecedented scales. In October 2004 when the 7th Buddhist Friendship Exchange Conference was co-held in China, South Korea and Japan, a decision was made in Beijing by eight Buddhist leaders from these three places across the Straits: to hold a World Buddhist Forum in China to improve real life, purify the mind, enlighten people and maintain peace. The planned forum was targeted at Buddhist disciples as well as those spiritual friends who care for and respect Buddhism. On April 13, 2006 senior monks from 37 countries and areas attended the First World Buddhism Forum; three years later, the Second World Buddhist Forum was held in March 28, 2009, attracting more than 1,700 senior Buddhist monks from about 50 countries and regions.

Tibetan Buddhism

Tibetan Language Buddhism is also called Tibetan Buddhism. In the 7th century AD, Buddhism entered Tibet in China and Tibetan Buddhism gradually took shape through interactions with the local Bon religion in Tibet. In the 13th century AD, Kublai Khan, the emperor of Yuan Dynasty (reigned 1260–1294), honored Basiba (1235–1280) as Royal Preceptor, and began to establish the governance system of alliance between church and state in Tibet. By the end of the 14th century, Tsongkhapa (1357–1419) founded the Geluk sect, which gradually became the most dominant sect of Tibetan Buddhism. The monks of the Geluk sect have also been traditionally known as the "Yellow Hats," because their ceremonial headdresses are yellow.

Under the system of alliance between church and state, temples in Tibet have abundant production materials and wealth, and most of the senior monks are government officials at different levels. Temples also have courts, prisons and instruments of torture.

After the founding of the PRC, the Chinese government carried out democratic reform in Tibet from 1959 to 1960, which abolished the serfdom of alliance between church and state. However, democratic reforms in Tibetan Buddhist temples only abolished those unreasonable old regulations. For example, temples are not allowed to interfere in administration, justice and marriage; temples, without permission, are not allowed to appoint officials and establish courts and prisons; people's personal bondage to temples are abolished; behaviors such as practicing usury and apportioning duties are forbidden in temples; the hierarchical management system in temples and the affiliation between the parent temple and subsidiary temples are repealed; through democratic election, Buddhist monks could establish committees or groups responsible for democratic management to deal with religious affairs on its own.

The country fully respects and protects the religious freedom of Tibetan citizens.

Tibetan Buddhism was introduced into the Mongol minority at the end of 16th century, which had a tremendous impact on Mongolian social life. In addition, Tibetan Buddhism also spread into the Monba, Tu, Qiang, and the Yugur

Lamas are having a debate over Buddhist scripture.

minorities, whose people become Tibetan Buddhists, too.

Tibetan Buddhism now has more than 3,000 temples, 120,000 monks and nuns, and over 1,700 Living Buddhas. The Lhasa Jokhang Temple with a long history was listed on the World Heritage List by UNESCO in 2000. The Geluk School has six famous temples—Gandan Temple, Sera Temple and Drepung Temple all in Lhasa, Tashilhunpo Temple in Shigatse, Tar Temple in Qinghai and Labrang Temple in Gansu. Yonghegong Lama Temple in Beijing and Puning Temple in Chengde in Hebei Province are important temples of Tibetan Buddhism in inland China.

The reincarnation of Living Buddha is a system adopted by Tibetan Buddhist temples to solve the problem of leadership succession. It was first created by the Karma Kagyu sect in the 13th century and then was gradually accepted by other sects.

The Living Buddha is identified with strict procedures. Living Buddhas always leave words before their death to predict the place where his reincarnated soul boy is born; if not, Buddhist monks will get inspiration through divination and séances.

According to clues provided in the last words, indications, signs, oracles and mirages on the lake, temples with the lineage of the Living Buddha send monks to different destinations, searching for supernatural children who were born after the Living Buddha passes away. There may be more than one candidate for the reincarnated soul boy, but only one is selected eventually.

The Dalai Lama and Bainqen Erdini are two Living Buddhas with the highest positions in the Geluk sect. In 1653, the fifth Dalai Lama was conferred a title by the central government of the Qing Dynasty. Afterwards, every reincarnation of the Dalai Lama should be bestowed a title by successive central governments, which became a fixed rule.

In 1713 the central government of the Qing Dynasty offered a title to the fifth Bainqen Erdini. From then onwards, every reincarnation of the Bainqen Erdini should also be honored by central governments.

In history, *Chuizhong* (the lama protecting and maintaining the Buddha dharma) was once in charge of identifying the reincarnated soul boy of the Living Buddha by casting a spell and asking the gods at a séance. However, some of them practiced fraud, and as a result, many of the reincarnated soul boys came from royal and aristocratic families, and thus religious power was manipulated by upper nobility or senior lamas. In 1793, the government of the Qing Dynasty issued regulations which provided the system of drawing lot from the golden urn. The method went like this: ivory slips, on which were the names and birthdays of soul boy candidates, were put into a golden urn and then the one whose name was on the drawn lot was identified as reincarnated soul boy. This was implemented on the premise that the whole process was supervised by representatives of the central government. Therefore, two urns were specially designed for drawing lots by the government of the Qing Dynasty: one was used to select the reincarnated soul boys of Living Buddha in the Tibetan area, such as the Dalai Lama and Bainqen Erdini, and is currently housed in the Potala Palace; the other is used for the selection of the Living Buddha in the Mongolian area, which is now housed in the Yonghegong Lama Temple in Beijing.

Since then, the system of drawing lot from the golden urn became a fixed rule and remains in operation today.

On January 28, 1989, the 10th Panchen Lama passed away in Tibet. The Chinese government announced the mission to locate and identify the reincarnated soul boy of the 10th Panchen Lama according to historical conventions and etiquettes of Tibetan Buddhism. It took six years to search for candidates, and three children were picked out. On November 29, 1995 by the lot-drawing method, Gyancain Norbu, a six-year-old boy, was confirmed as the reincarnated soul boy of the 10th Panchen Erdeni.

Pali Buddhism

Pali Buddhism is also known as Hinayana Buddhism, or "Theravada Buddhism." Around the 7th century AD, Theravada Buddhism was introduced into Yunnan Province. The religion first exerted influence on the Dai minority in Xishuangbanna and Dehong, which made every member of the Dai minority a Theravada Buddhist. After that, Theravada Buddhism gradually spread among the Blang, Achang and De'ang minorities, making most of them believers in Theravada Buddhism.

Monks of the Dai minority are holding religious activities.

The Dai minority has fully integrated their life with Theravada Buddhism. In almost every village in Dai area are clean and solemn temples as well as beautiful white pagodas. The Dai people once wrote Buddhist scriptures down on pattra leaves in the old Dai language, leaving behind a precious cultural heritage. Historically, monastic education is an important form of education in the Dai minority. In their tradition, a boy at the age of seven or eight must become a monk and learn in Buddhist temples not only about Buddhist scriptures but also secular culture. After a period of learning, ranging from several months to several years, most of them resume secular life, while the rest stay in Buddhist temples.

The Blang, De'ang, and Achang minorities are all pious believers in Theravada Buddhism, although they have their own ancient style of worship. In the villages of the Blang and De'ang minorities, Buddhist temples and pagodas are everywhere.

Nowadays, in China, Pali Buddhism has nearly 10,000 bhikshus and elders, and more than 1,600 Buddhist temples.

Taoism

Lao-tzu (about 580–500 BC) was revered as father of Taoism for his contribution to later Taoism. His concepts laid the foundation of Taoism. It is noteworthy that distinctions should be made between Taoism which was established in the 2nd century AD and the Taoist philosophy of Lao-tzu , although *Tao Te Ching* written by Lao-tzu was regarded as a classic by successive leaders of Taoism in later ages.

The civil groups "Peace Avenue" and "Five Pecks of Rice" in the Eastern Han Dynasty marked the formation of Taoism. The publication of *Tai Ping Classic, Zhouyi Cantong Qi*

Baopu Taoist temple in Hangzhou, Zhejiang.

(Three Ways Unified and Normalized of the Book of Changes) and *Lao-tzu Xiang'er Zhu (Xiang Er's Annotation on Lao Tzu)* indicated the formation of Taoist belief and theories. Most Chinese scholars tend to believe that although Taoist doctrines contain an element of Taoist culture of Lao-tzu, it is far from representing the spirit of Taoism and Lao-tzu.

Taoism believes: *Tao* is the essence of everything; *Tao* is the ultimate reality, a presence that existed before the universe was formed and that continues to guide the world and everything in it; society and human life should follow *Tao*; when human beings follow the rules of *Tao* and concentrate on self-cultivation, they can eventually achieve peace of mind, build their bodies, eliminate disease, prolong life, and even become immortal. The utmost goal of Taoism is to achieve immortality through life cultivation.

Many religious doctrines believe that life is full of pain; however, life is a source of joy for Taoist, and they encourage people to enjoy their lives. Therefore, Taoism developed after many mysterious methods of life cultivation, such

Taoist activities in Baiyunguan Temple, Beijing.

as spiritual practice, food practice, breathing practice and physical practice, among which the most amazing one is *Dan Tao*.

Dan Tao includes external *Dan* and internal *Dan*. The former one refers to pills of immortality that Taoists made by smelting minerals like cinnabar and plumbum in stoves and bronze tripods. This cultivation method reached its zenith in the Tang Dynasty, followed by a gradual decline, and was replaced by external *Dan*. The latter one means that Taoists use their bodies as "stoves and bronze tripods," by the methods of exhaling and inhaling of breath, to make energy gathered into pills of immortality inside human bodies; the success of *Dan*-making help Taoists become immortal.

No matter whether there are any immortals by the method of external *Dan* or internal *Dan*, it is undeniable that external *Dan* and internal *Dan* have objectively made an unexpected contribution to Chinese culture: external *Dan* resulted in the achievements in metallurgy and chemistry in China, even leading to the invention of gunpowder; while internal *Dan* has greatly contributed to health science in China. For instance, the practice of *qigong* (a breathing exercise) is very popular in today's China which benefits people's health.

The "paradise" that Taoists yearn for does not entirely equal purely imaginary heaven and it also exists on earth. On earth, lands governed by gods are known as *Dongtianfudi* (cave of heavens and lands of happiness). Taoism points out there are 10 cave heavens, 36 small cave heavens, and 72 lands of happiness in China. These *Dongtianfudi* are all located in famous mountains and great rivers, have many historical Taoist temples as well as historical sites where legendary immortals are said to be practicing out there. Nowadays, these scenic spots of great heritage value have become popular destinations for Chinese tourists. Some of the scenic spots have been listed by UNESCO on the World Heritage

List, such as Qingcheng Mountain in Sichuan known as "the 5th Cave Heaven," Wuyi Mountain in Fujian known as "the 16th Cave Heaven," Wudang Mountain in Hubei known as "the 9th Land of Happiness" and Lushan Mountain in Jiangxi known as "the 71st Land of Happiness."

A Taoist priest is a person who takes part in Taoist activities as his profession. A Taoist temple is the place where Taoist activities are held. In the 12th century, after the rise of the famous Quanzhen sect in Taoism, Taoist temples began to learn from Buddhist temples about temple management.

The Chinese Taoist Association was founded in 1957 and located in the White Cloud Temple in Beijing. It is the first unified association in the history of China that has included all Taoists. In addition, there are 133 Taoist organizations at all levels throughout the country. In 1990, the Chinese Taoism Association set up the China Taoist Academy, the first nationwide Taoist academy in the history of Chinese Taoism.

Islam

The Tang Dynasty was a great and open dynasty which encouraged foreign merchants to do business in China. Due to advanced external transport, more than 70 foreign countries traded with China during this period. At that time, a large number of Arabian and Persian merchants came to China. Attracted by the prosperous economy and tolerant atmosphere of politics and culture, some of them stayed in China, got married and had children, and worked for the royal government after having passed the imperial examinations.

These Arabian and Persian merchants, known as *Fanke* (foreign guests) in China, were the first group of people that brought Islam to China.

The second crucial stage of the spread and development

of Islam in China was during the Yuan Dynasty. During the 50 years from the beginning of the 13th century, in a large-scale Mongolian westward expansion, a group of Arabs, Persians and Central Asians were conscripted for the war against the Song Dynasty in China. These people, together with the descendants of the Arabs and Persians were called Huis people.

Because Huis people lived together and intermarried with Han people and Mongolians for quite a long time, by the the late Yuan and early Ming dynasties, a new ethnic group had finally been formed, that is, the Hui minority. The formation of the Hui minority laid a stable social foundation for the spread of Islam in China. Meanwhile, it also indicated that Islamic believers were no longer immigrants, and after living here for as long as 700 or 800 years, their descendants became native Chinese ethnic

A Muslim temple in Kashi, Xinjiang.

minorities. This also transformed Islam from a foreign religion into one which was rooted in China and has become an important part of Chinese culture.

The Chinese language is commonly used in the Hui minority, while the Arabic and Persian languages are usually used in religious activities. As for when and how these Muslims lost their original languages, some scholars explain that because there were few women among merchants and soldiers, they had to marry local women of the Han ethnic group in order to have children. Then passed down from mother to son, people of the Hui minority gradually became familiar with their mothers' language, Han Chinese, and eventually adopted it. Furthermore, they mastered Chinese for the purpose of trading. In fact, the Hui minority has integrated Islamic ethics with a traditional Chinese concept of "respect for God and ancestors" in aspects of ethics and code of conduct; as to a religious education system, the Hui minority has combined the Islamic monastic education with

An Iman is preaching Islamic doctrines.

the traditional private school education in China, which forms the unique "Mosque Education" in Chinese Islam.

Islamic localization in China made further progress in the Qing Dynasty: some scholars not only explained Islamic doctrines, disciplines, decrees and regulations in the Chinese language, but also dedicated themselves to the combination of Confucian and Islamic doctrines. During the same period, Islamic sects and the Menhuan system with Chinese characteristics were formed in Chinese Islam. Menhuan was the product of Islamic mysticism (Sufism) and patriarchal system in China. What's more, mosque architecture at that time began to integrate with the traditional Chinese architectural style; the family lives of all Chinese Muslims also started to melt into the traditional Chinese etiquette in daily life.

Islam began to spread in Xinjiang as early as the 10th century AD. Before that, the ethnic groups here were all pious believers of Buddhism, which has a history of over 1,000 years in Xinjiang. Actually, as a crucial route on the Silk Road, around 1 AD, Xinjiang accommodated many important religions in the world, including Shamanism, Manichaeism, Nestorianism, and Zoroastrianism. Uygur people used to be believers of the above-mentioned religions as well as Buddhism. After the spread of Islam for more than four centuries and the Islamic religious war against Buddhism, Islam was finally accepted by the Uygur minority. Islam was not accepted by other ethnic minorities in Xinjiang until the 18th century.

There are mainly 10 Muslim ethnic groups in China. Besides the Hui and Uygur minorities, they also include the Kazak, Kirgiz, Ozbek, Tatar and Tajik minorities in Xinjiang; the Salar minority in Qinghai; the Dongxiang minority and the Bonan minority in Gansu.

At present, there are over 34,000 mosques in China. This indicates that in China, for every 600 Muslims of the 20 million have a mosque. Many of these mosques were restored or newly built in the 1980s.

The Islamic Association of China was founded in Beijing in 1953, serving as a nationwide organization of Islam in China; its association journal, Chinese Muslims is published in both Chinese and Uygur. Some provinces, autonomous regions and municipalities where Muslims live in compact communities all have their own Islamic associations as well as publications.

China has now published the *Koran* in 10 languages to meet the needs of Muslim readers among various ethnic groups.

Currently, China has 11 Islamic academies for mosque education. China Islamic Institute, founded in Beijng in 1955, is the highest institution of learning in Chinese Islam.

Catholicism

In 1294, The Franciscan missionary John of Montecorvino (1247–1328) arrived in the capital of the Yuan Dynasty and received the government's permission to establish Catholic churches, which marked the introduction of Catholicism into China. However, with the fall of the Yuan Dynasty, Catholicism withered away in the country.

In the 16th century, with the expansion of Western colonialism, Catholicism again entered China. During this period, Matteo Ricci (1552–1610), an Italian Jesuit missionary, laid the foundation for Catholicism in China.

Speaking of Matteo Ricci, many Chinese people view him as an important figure in the cultural communication between East and West, rather than a Catholic missionary. His huge success in China was due to his flexible adaptation to Chinese culture.

Before setting foot on the mainland of China, Matteo

Catholic Church in Wangfujing, Beijing.

Ricci first learned Chinese in Macao. In 1583, he arrived in Guangdong, where he made friends with Chinese officials and men of letters; even his daily life was localized. He once shaved his head, wore the monastic habit, and called himself a "Western monk;" then he took off his cassock, let his beard and hair grow, and wore Confucian clothing. This change resulted from his one discovery, that Confucianism really dominates China. Thus, he began to study Confucian teachings, and even translated Confucian classics, attempting to reconcile Confucianism with Catholicism.

Although people speak highly of Matteo Ricci, he actually spread Catholicism in China.

In 1601, Matteo Ricci came to Beijng, and was received by the then emperor. Ricci's extensive knowledge won the respect and appreciation of the Chinese emperor. He got the permission from the emperor to do missionary work, and was granted an official position, making him an official of the Ming Dynasty. Thereafter, Catholicism secured a place in China.

By the time Matteo Ricci passed away in 1610 in China, there had been more than 2,000 baptized Christians in the country.

In 1637, China had over 40,000 Catholics. The Vatican decided to implement a Vicar Apostolic in China, entrusting missionaries from Spain, France and Italy with missionary districts in China. Three colonial empires struggled fiercely for missionary influence in China.

Tributes to Confucius and ancestors are Chinese traditions with a long history. Matteo Ricci once proposed to adapt to this practice in China. However, after Spanish and French missionary organizations entered China, the heated debate over whether to tolerate this practice began. It became known as "the Chinese Rites Controversy" in the history of Catholicism. After swaying between two opinions, Vatican eventually forbade Chinese Catholics to practice traditional Chinese rites and sent special envoys to implement that decree.

This move caused the Catholic Church to lose the support of many intellectuals in China, and widened the gap between Chinese elite culture and Catholicism in particular. Owing to the Vatican's negative attitude towards Chinese rites, Emperor Kangxi (reigned 1662–1722) of the Qing Dynasty banned Catholicism in China, which lasted for over 100 years.

When the Opium War broke out in 1840, Western powers used gunboats to pry open the doors of China. Soon after that, the Chinese government was forced to sign a series of unequal treaties and to repeal its ban against Catholicism. The Sino-France Beijing Treaty in 1860 stipulated the Qing government should return and compensate previously seized Catholic property. A French missionary serving as a translator added an article to the treaty without permission in the process of translation, which provided that, "French missionaries are allowed to rent or purchase land and to construct estates as they wish." This Treaty indicated that France had gained a political privilege that gave an all-round protection to Catholicism. Meanwhile, after more than 10 years of diplomatic negotiations, the Vatican and the government of Portugal finally reached an agreement to turn the mission fields in Beijing and Nanjing that once belonged under Portugal patronage into French mission fields. After the 1880s, German and Italy, through military power, also gained the same privilege from the Chinese government.

During this period, relying on colonial forces, Catholic missionaries acquired political privileges enjoyed by dukes of medieval churches which had long been abolished in Western Europe. In 1899, the Qing government was forced to issue "Rules for Reception of Missionaries by Local Officials," officially admitting that Catholic Bishops enjoyed a political status equivalent to that of a governor-general and inspector-general; the General Secretary of the Church was equal to the status of *Sidao*; while missionaries were the equivalent of state and county officials.

The consecration ceremony for seminarians in National Seminary of the Chinese Catholic Church.

During the same period, conflicts arose between Catholicism and Chinese society. The main reasons were that some missionaries purchased or took possession of land by force; some viewed themselves as winners, and interfered with local government affairs and litigation. Under these circumstances, the Boxer Uprising broke out on a grand scale, and later swept across the northern provinces in China. The Boxer Uprising was an anti-imperialist and patriotic movement with Chinese farmers as the main group; it was also an overwhelming outbreak of all the conflicts between Catholicism, Protestantism and Chinese people during the last half-century.

This movement made the Catholic Church aware of its own problems. The Vatican began to ban missionaries from interfering in litigations of Chinese Catholics, and churches from intervening in political and diplomatic activities; meanwhile, the Vatican began enhancing its social influence by running schools, practicing medicine and participating in charities. From then on, Catholicism developed at a faster speed in China.

By 1949, there were 3.18 million Catholics in China.

However, the Vatican refused to accept the newly founded the People's Republic of China. Some people in the Catholic Church took an anti-communist stance and forbade followers to join any organizations led by the Chinese government; some even collected information about China in the guise of priests.

Under such circumstances, in November 1950, a Chinese priest Wang Liangzuo in Guangyuan county of Sichuan Province together with over 500 Catholics issued Three-Self Declarations, calling for a Catholic Church of self-governance, self-support, and self-propagation. This appeal was followed by repercussions among Catholics, and shortly afterwards, Catholics in other places made similar statements. In 1957, the Chinese Patriotic Catholic Association was founded.

The resolution adopted by the first Catholic Congress stated, "To maintain a purely religious relationship with

Vatican City on the premise that no one violates the interests and independent dignity of the country; to obey the Pope's teachings that are creditable and practical; and to cut off political and economic ties with Vatican City."

Around 1949, many missionaries left mainland China willingly, while some were deported for anti-China activities. There were only some 20 bishops in 137 mission fields nationwide, which greatly hindered the development of Catholic activities in China. In March 1958, the Hankou mission field and Wuchang mission field in Hubei selected Dong Guangqing (1917–2007) and Yuan Wenhua (1905–1973) as bishop candidates respectively, and asked the Vatican's approval for the consecration date by telegram. However, the Vatican sent a telegram in reply, saying that bishops selected by themselves were invalid; due to whatever ritual or status, if a bishop consecrates a "bishop" without the nomination or approval of the Holy See, consecrators and consecratees were both subject to "super-excommunication."

The Chinese Catholic Church was thrown into a dilemma: the Vatican's ban on the one hand, and needs of Chinese Catholics for a normal religious life on the other hand. It had no choice but to select and consecrate bishops by themselves. This method was determined then and has continued to this day.

Although the Catholic Church in China adheres to the principle of independence, self-management does not mean that it refuses all contact and communication with Catholic churches around the world. In fact, since the founding of the PRC, especially since the reform and opening up, the Chinese Catholic Bishops College and mission fields throughout the country have received a large number of Catholic clergies from around the world, among whom many are well-known religious leaders.

In return, the Chinese Catholic Church has also received invitations to visit Catholic churches all over the world, and to attend events such as the World Conference on Religion and Peace.

Currently, the number of Catholics in China has jumped to more than 5 million from over 3 million at the initial stage of the founding of the PRC. The Chinese Catholic Academy of Theology and Philosophy was established in 1983. It is a national Roman Catholic seminary under the direct management of the Chinese Catholic Bishops College, with a six-year school system, serving as highest institution of Catholicism in China and theological research center.

Protestantism

Robert Morrison (1782–1834), a British missionary, arrived in China in 1807, marking China's first encounter with Protestantism. Due to the Qing government's ban on the spread of Catholicism and Protestantism, Morrison and other missionaries who arrived in China later could only do missionary work in secrecy along the southeast coastal area.

The Opium War in 1840 opened China's doors. By the end of the 19th century, there were about 1,500 Protestant missionaries with around 80,000 followers in China.

Protestantism entered China together with the colonial invasion of Western powers. Therefore, many Chinese people linked the spread of Protestantism with the ancient country's decline and fall, betrayal and humiliation. Jiang Menglin (1886–1964), president of Peking University in the 1920s, provided an explanation: "When a religion is connected with military power, its image will definitely be changed. And when it comes to Protestantism, it is also inevitable for people to connect it with intimidation by

force. Gradually, people get the idea that Tathagata came to China by riding on a white elephant, while Jesus Christ flew to China on artillery shells."

Under the protection of unequal treaties, some Protestant missionaries had nothing to fear in China. That belief frequently led to conflicts and disputes between the populace and Western missionaries, which was called "Church Case" in the history. From 1840 to 1900, there were more than 400 church cases all over China. Various "Church Cases" became the excuse for Western powers to make further demands to the Chinese government and even wage a war of aggression which led to the Boxer Uprising.

With large-scale bloody conflicts, the Protestant Church suffered a serious setback in China, forcing Protestants

Shanghai International Chapel in Hengshan, built in 1920, is the biggest Christian church in Shanghai.

to restrain their behavior. Some missionaries began to realize that missionary methods should be reformed to reduce Chinese people's resentment and resistance to foreign missionaries. The new method was to run in schools, hospitals and charitable institutions rather than preach people directly.

When Western missionaries set about practicing the new missionary strategy, China was entering a new era where the decline of the country caused profound cultural reflections; it became a major cause in society that in order to save the nation from doom, and Chinese people strove for self-support and innovation, and accepted Western culture consciously or unconsciously. That was golden opportunity to spread Protestantism.

By 1922, the number of Protestants in China had increased to about 400,000, and by 1949, there were almost 700,000.

The Protestant Church not only delivered sermons in China's large cities, but also established churches in remote and rural places. Meanwhile, it continued with the Self-support Movement and Indegenouzation Movement. The Self-support Movement started from the 1870s, while at that time, the development of Protestantism was hindered, which concerned some people in Chinese Protestant churches. They were keen for an independent Protestant Church with Chinese characteristics by changing people's impression of Protestantism as a "foreign religion" and establishing churches by themselves.

In the beginning, the Movement of Self-support was a merely spontaneous action by some Chinese Protestants. By the 20th century, it had developed into a church movement. In 1922, the National Christian Conference of China was held in Shanghai, which set up a national organization—the National Christian Council of China. This organization put forth the slogan of establishing an indigenous church, and advocated that followers in China should assume responsibilties and promote traditional Chinese culture in order to remove the title "foreign religion" from Protestanism.

The Indegenouzation Movement of Chinese Protestants aimed to make Protestantism indigenous. It was characterized by the following points: opposing total Westernization; advocating combining with traditional Chinese culture in aspects of doctrines, organizations and rites; carrying forward the inherent Chinese culture while maintaining a certain degree of cooperation with the Western Church.

In reality, however, it was not easy to integrate Protestantism into Chinese culture. After proposing the Indegenouzation Movement, Chinese Protestants made efforts in practice by adopting the architecture style of Chinese temples when constructing churches and singing hymns in folk tunes. Obviously, that was only integration in form; people were still uncertain about how to integrate Protestantism with the essence of Chinese culture.

Students from Nanjing Union Theological Seminary.

After the founding of the PRC in 1949, although New China advocated religious freedom, many religious followers still held a skeptical attitude and sensed a gloomy prospect due to anti-communist propaganda by some foreign missionaries. At this point in time, some men with foresight in Protestant churches realized only if Chinese Christianity purged the past impact of Western powers and completed a self-transformation to match with the changing Chinese society could it make new progress.

For this reason, in September 23, 1950, 40 leading figures from various religious denominations headed by Wu Yaozong published the "Three-Self Declaration," in the title of "The Way in Which Chinese Christianity Works for New China's Construction." It requested all Protestants in China to achieve the "Three-Self" (self-governance, self-support and self-propagation) of Chinese churches as soon as possible. That marked the start of "Three-Self" Reform of the Protestant Church in China.

The Declaration was met with enthusiastic responses from patriotic Protestants. By 1954, more than 410,000 followers had signed up to uphold the Declaration, accounting for two-thirds of the total Protestants in China.

In 1954 the First National Conference of the Chinese Christian Church, held in Beijing, established the National Committee of the Three-Self Patriotic Movement of the Protestant Churches in China with Wu Yaozong as chairman.

The "Three-Self Movement," to some extent, marked that Protestantism in China was transformed into China's own religion from a foreign religion.

Protestant churches in China have sought self-governance, self-support, and self-propagation, but this does not mean self-isolation. Over 50 years since the founding of the PRC, Protestant churches in China have established formal relationships with Protestant organizations in many countries; they have hosted overseas visiting groups, organized delegations for visits abroad and attended international conferences of Protestantism. In 1991, the China Christian Council officially joined the World Council of Churches.

After reform and opening up, Protestantism developed at a fantastic speed. In 1979, there were more than 3 million followers; by 2002, the number had surged to over 16 million with nearly 50,000 churches.

It was once reported by foreign media that there was an acute shortage of *The Holy Bible* in China. But as a matter of fact, from 1988 to the end of 2002, China published 30 million Bibles in various languages, such as Chinese, English, Korean, Miao language, Jingpo language, Lahu language, Kawa language, Lisu language and Yi language. In some ethnic regions, most Bibles are given to followers at no charge. Amity Development Co., Ltd. in Nanjing specializes in printing *The Bible*. It is a joint venture between United Bible Societies and The Amity Foundation that was set up in 1987.

Apart from the National Committee of the Three-Self Patriotic Movement of the Protestant Churches in China, the China Christian Council, founded in 1980, is another nationwide Protestant organization. The two organizations are located in Shanghai. Throughout China, there are various local Three-Self patriotic associations and Protestant associations, amounting to more than 1,700.

China has 17 Christian theological seminaries. The Nanjing Union Theological Seminary, established in 1952, is a nationwide theological seminary in China.

The Policy of Religious Freedom in China

In a country governed by an atheist party, can theistic religions be tolerated and accepted? Generally speaking, current religious policies in China mainly include the following points:

(1) Citizens enjoy the freedom to believe or not to believe in religion. One has the right to believe in any sect out of their own choice, to express one's own religious belief and religious identity.

(2) The country follows the principles of decoupling religion

Religious committees attending the National Political Consultative Conference.

from politics. No religion is allowed to interfere in government administrative and judicial systems; the government is not allowed to interfere in the internal affairs of religions, and no single religion is granted a special position.

(3) Religious organizations must act within the scope of the Constitution as well as relevant laws and policies. When exercising the right of religious freedom, no individual should use religion as a pretext for doing harm to the country, society and individuals. The country protects religious activities in line with the Constitution, relevant laws and policies. The country protects the legitimate rights and interests of religious organizations as well as the rights of professional religious personnel performing religious duties.

(4) All religions are equal. The government provides equal treatment to all religions; all religions are politically and legally equal regardless of the number of believers and influence.

(5) Mutual respect should be built between atheism and theism. In China, because non-believers are in the majority, the government stipulates religious activities should be carried out in religious venues. No individual is permitted to conduct atheist propaganda in religious venues, or to launch a debate on theism and atheism among religious believers; no religious organizations are allowed to sermon, preach and publicize theism beyond religious venues.

(6) All religions in China shall follow the principles of independence and self-management, and shall develop mutual exchanges and cooperation with overseas religious

In September 2003, the 50th anniversary of the establishment of the Buddhist Association of China was held in Beijing.

organizations and personages on the basis of equality and friendliness. The country never allows foreign countries to interfere in China's internal affairs in the name of religion.

A Village Story: Peaceful Coexistence among Different Religions in Contemporary Society

Bingzhongluo is located in the upper reaches of the Nu-jiang River, where A-Nong, a branch of the Nu minority, thrives here. As the Tibetan and Lisu minorities moved to Bingzhongluo from north and south respectively, A-Nong people gradually had neighbors and relatives from these two ethnic groups. They purchased Lisu ironware and Ti-betan butter buckets and meanwhile added supernatural be-liefs of Lisu and Tibetan Buddhism to their primitive beliefs. In modern times, Catholism and Christianity (Protestantism) in the Western world came to China one after another. After experiencing a series of painful experiences, A-Nong people claimed to have seen "Jesus" and "Maria."

He Lin is a doctor working in a research institute of ethnic minorities at Yunnan University as well as in a research cen-ter for ethnic minorities in the southwest frontier. In 2005, He Lin stayed for 12 month in the village where A-Nong people live. Here, he made an in-depth observation and re-search on a phenomenon—the peaceful coexistence among different religious beliefs of ethnic minorities in Yunnan in contemporary society.

The following is his story about Bingzhongluo (Bijionglo in Tibetan pronunciation, Manbiekong in A-Nong pronun-ciation).

Peach blossoms bloom in the spring of Bingzhongluo. Ancient lamaseries, Protestant Churches and Catholic churches are located no more than 1 kilometer away from each other. During festivals—no matter the festivals of

A Buddhist temple in rural Yunnan.

lamasery, Catholic Church or Protestant Church, the winding mountain roads are full of well-dressed people, including the A-Nong people, Tibetan people and Lisu people. Shuangla village is a village in Bingzhongluo. Here a Protestant Church and a Catholic church face each other across the river; while Songdebu [in Tibetan culture, it is a place where believers of Lamaism offer sacrifices to gods] are scattered around stone bungalows surrounded by barley land, which marks the religious beliefs of house owners. However, it may not be completely correct to judge the belief of a household just by Songdebu and Lama Stamp surrounding the house, cross painted on the door, or Madonna in the house. Because you may see two or even three of these signs in many households; sometimes you may see none of these signs in a household, but its family members may have different religious beliefs.

If people describe the paradise in their hearts as a "harmonious coexistence between man and nature," then in the paradise of A-Nong people, there is still mutual tolerance and harmony between man and man, man and god, god and god. People are curious of how to achieve a "harmonious coexistence" among different religious beliefs, and among different ethnic minorities.

By the end of 2004, Bingzhongluo had a population of 6,205, among which there were 3,159 A-Nong people, 2,027 Lisu people, 520 Tibetan people and 305 Dulong people. The number of religious believers here was 3,887, accounting for 63 percent of the total population.

The self-claimed "A-Nong" people belong to the Nu minority. People of the Nu minority are ancient inhabitants in the areas around the Nujiang River and are named after this river. A-Nong people speak the A-Nong language with no written language, but almost all the people here understand Lisu language and Tibetan language, and more and more people are proficient in Chinese language.

Tibetan Buddhism entered Bingzhongluo in 1733, which soon became the main religion here. Catholicism was introduced by French missionaries in 1889. At that time, the spread of Catholicism here triggered a violent religious conflict. Due to repression from the Qing Dynasty government and the then Western imperialist powers, Catholicism finally gained a foothold. Christianity was introduced in 1930 by American missionaries and spread fast.

What do A-Nong people think when facing so many religions?

In history, A-Nong people used legends to explain their relations with Lisu people, Tibetan people, Dulong people and Han people who were also their neighbors and relatives. The ancient legend said, these ethnic minorities were all brothers and sisters who had the same Moon father and the same Sun mother. Subsequently, A-Nong people used a new legend to explain the relations among various religions.

The new legend said, Tibetan Buddhism and Catholicism, Christianity are "brothers and sisters of a family."

This legend goes like this: a long time ago, the religions of A-Nong are a family. They came from India, moved to Tibet later and lived at the foot of Kawagebo Hill. There were four children in this family, but they did not get along well. Then the eldest son went to Jinshajiang River and became Buddhism (Chinese Buddhism); the second son stayed in Tibet and became Lamaism (Tibetan Buddhism); one of the two stubborn daughters was put into a bag by their mother and thrown into the Lancang River, and then drifted to a place called France; the other one was thrown into the Nujiang River and reached the United Kingdom. After a period of time, the two daughters came back: one was Catholicism, who called herself Maria and was later rescued by a Tibetan caravan, and thus Catholicism began to spread first in the Tibetan minority; the other one became Christianity (Protestantism) who drifted to the place where Lisu people live, and therefore Christianity was first spread among the Lisu minority.

In this legend, A-Nong people use family ties to explain the relations among different religions; and they use scenes in a family to describe the memories of the conflicts and fights among different religions in the past and to express a desire for a harmonious coexistence in the future.

Tuesday is market day in Bingzhongluo. Speaking different languages, people feel free to trade, talk, eat and drink. Although they almost dress the same way, you can still distinguish their religious beliefs in a short time: a person with a circle of woolen thread (red or multicolored) around the neck should be a Tibetan Buddhist; a person without a circle of woolen thread around neck but a tobacco pipe in the mouth or drinks in hand may be a Catholic; a person, who solely drinks soft drinks rather than smoke or drink beer,

A centennial Catholic church in Cizhong village, Deqin county, Yunnan.

should be a Christian...

As a matter of fact, the ancient primitive religion—nature worship, still exists among A-Nong people; relevant priests are called *Nanmusa,* or sorcerers.

Zhao Guoqiang's family have the most religious beliefs: the eldest son and second son are Catholics and they go to church every Sunday; his youngest daughter believes in Tibetan Buddhism with her husband; while his wife and daughter-in-law believe in Christianity, and go to church every Wednesday evening and Sunday. Zhao Guoqiang himself has no religious belief, and thus he goes nowhere but stays at home to farm.

Religions here are not in contact with one another. And there is no connection with religious ceremonies between Catholicism and Christianity, even though the two are of the same origin. Then, under this circumstance, how can close relationships be established among believers of different religions? Surely, in Bingzhongluo, it would never happen that a Christian goes to a Catholic church or a Catholic goes to a Protestant Church, or that a Christian and a Catholic participate in Lamas' chanting. Catholic priests and Christian pastors here all say they have no religious connections, and even no cooperation with regards to Christmas activities. However, when the Catholic Church was established there in 1996, congratulatory gifts were sent by the Protestant Church in Shuangla village—A-Nong people often help each other or congratulate relatives and neighbors in this way. This shows that A-Nong people make a clear distinction between religion and daily life, and nobody likes to meddle in other people's matters.

A-Nong people would never have two or more than two religious beliefs. They are loyal to their own beliefs. Due to the unforgettable memories of disharmony among "brothers and sisters" in the legend and a desire for a peaceful life, A-Nong people are always striving for a harmonious coexistence among different religions.